you can RENEW this item from home by visiting our Website at www.woodbridge.lioninc.org or by calling (203) 389-3433

7/04

REFERENCE

Life & Times in 20th-Century America

America

Volume 5: Promise and Change

1981–2000

Greenwood Publishing Group

Library of Congress Cataloging-in-Publication Data

Life & times in 20th-century America / by Media Projects, Inc.

    p. cm

      Includes bibliographical references and indexes.

  Contents: v. 1. Becoming a modern nation, 1900-1920 — v. 2. Boom times, hard times,
1921-1940 — v. 3. Hot and cold wars, 1941-1960 — v. 4. Troubled times at home,
1961-1980 — v. 5. Promise and change, 1981-2000.

ISBN 0–313–32570–7 (set: alk. paper)—ISBN 0–313–32571–5 (v. 1: alk. paper) —
ISBN 0–313–32572–3 (v. 2: alk. paper)—ISBN 0–313–32573–1 (v. 3: alk. paper) —
ISBN 0–313-32574–X (v. 4: alk. paper)—ISBN 0–313–32575–8 (v. 5: alk. paper)

  1. United States—History—20th century. 2. United States—Social conditions—20th
century. 3. United States—Social life and customs—20th century. I. Media Projects
Incorporated.

E741.L497 2004

973.91—dc21   2003044829

British Library Cataloguing in Publication Data is available.

Library of Congress Catalog Card Number: 2003044829
ISBN: 0–313–32570–7 (set)
      0–313–32571–5 (vol. 1)
      0–313–32572–3 (vol. 2)
      0–313–32573–1 (vol. 3)
      0–313–32574–X (vol. 4)
      0–313–32575–8 (vol. 5)

First published in 2004

Greenwood Press, 88 Post Road West, Westport, CT 06881
An imprint of Greenwood Publishing Group, Inc.
www.greenwood.com

Printed in the United States of America

The paper used in this book complies with the
Permanent Paper Standard issued by the National
Information Standards Organization (Z39.48–1984).

10 9 8 7 6 5 4 3 2 1

Media Projects, Inc.
Managing Editor: Carter Smith
Writer: Dale Anderson
Editor: Carolyn Jackson
Production Editor: Jim Burmester
Indexer: Marilyn Flaig
Designer: Amy Henderson
Copy Editor: Elin Woodger

Contents

America Closes the Century

As the 1980s began, the United States faced several problems. The economy was stuck in a slump. The Cold War, begun after World War II between the United States and the communist Union of Soviet Socialist Republics (USSR), was flaring up again. Finally, fifty-three Americans were being held hostage in Iran. The nation was losing its confidence.

Twenty years later, the United States was in a completely different mood, confidently poised on the beginning of a new millennium, or period of a thousand years. The country was celebrating a long economic boom. The Cold War had ended, and the United States was the most powerful nation in the world, the only superpower. Even better, countries around the world looked to the United States as a model for its political and economic systems. What had happened?

An Economic Boom

One reason for the better mood was good economic news. In the 1970s, people struggled to get by. Jobs were scarce. Inflation sent prices soaring, making what money people had worth less than before. While many people still struggled in the 1980s and 1990s, large numbers of Americans were better off than they had ever been.

On taking office as president in 1981, Republican Ronald Reagan called for deep tax cuts. Congress lowered taxes by 25 percent, the largest cut in history. This put more money in consumers' pockets. Reagan increased defense spending sharply, which created jobs in defense industries. At the same time, oil prices fell. This helped lower inflation. Interest rates, which determine how much banks and other lenders charge for loans, dropped too.

CLOCKWISE: **A woman works at her personal computer (Fotosearch); Earth Day celebration, 1990** (Library of Congress); **Ronald Reagan (Center) with wife Nancy and Senator Strom Thurmond of South Carolina in 1984.** (Library of Congress)

This made it cheaper to borrow money. Consumers began to spend, and businesses produced more things for them to buy. The economy began to surge.

The percentage of people looking for work without success fell from 8.5 percent in 1975 to 7.1 percent in 1980 and 7.2 percent in 1985, before plummeting to 5.6 percent in 1990. By 2000, it was just 4 percent. The economic growth slowed briefly between 1991 and 1993. That sent the jobless rate up to around 7 percent before it headed down again.

The Consumer Price Index (CPI) measures the cost of goods and services in eight categories, such as housing, medical care, and food and beverages. By its measurements, prices rose 13.3 percent in 1979. That set a thirty-three year record not seen since the Great Depression. Prices rose another 13.5 percent the following year, and by 10.3 percent in 1981. They never grew that fast again for the rest of the century. The rate of growth in prices dropped to 3.6 percent in 1985, moved up to 5.4 percent in 1990, but was down to 2.8 percent in 1995 and 3.4 percent in 2000. The CPI had not been that low since 1960.

With lower inflation, people could buy more with their money. In addition, they were earning more. The average income for American families more than doubled between 1980 and the late 1990s.

Not all the economic signs were positive. Manufacturing workers lost more jobs as companies closed U.S. factories and built new ones overseas.

1981
Ronald Reagan is inaugurated as president after defeating Jimmy Carter in the 1980 election.

1981
President Reagan survives an assassination attempt when he is shot after delivering a speech in Washington.

The Reagan administration wins what is then the largest tax cut in American history, cutting taxes by 25 percent.

1981
President Reagan nominates Sandra Day O'Connor as a Supreme Court justice. After the U.S. Senate approves the nomination, O'Connor becomes the first woman to serve on the nation's highest court.

1982
The Vietnam Veterans Memorial is dedicated. It is designed by Maya Lin, a 22-year-old architecture student.

African Americans still suffered from higher unemployment and lower wages than whites. On the whole, though, the economy was in far better shape in 2000 than in 1980. Businesses were more productive, and Americans of all walks of life were enjoying good times. Nearly two-thirds of all Americans owned their own homes. Three-quarters of those homes had air conditioning. It took the average worker only 23 hours to earn enough to buy a color television—compared to 174 hours in 1970.

The End of the Cold War

Another reason for greater optimism in the 1990s was the end of the Cold War.

Throughout the 1970s, the United States had worked for better relations with the Soviet Union (the Union of Soviet Socialist Republics, or USSR). Late in 1979, though, the Soviet Union jeopardized that progress. It sent thousands of troops into the Asian country of Afghanistan to protect a communist government from Muslim rebels. President Jimmy Carter was outraged. He pulled from the Senate a treaty aimed at limiting U.S. and Soviet nuclear arms. He blocked the sale of American wheat and high-technology products to the Soviet Union. He demanded that the United States boycott, or stay out of, the Olympic Games held in Moscow in 1980. The boycott was intended to keep Soviet leaders and their nation out of the international spotlight.

1982

After communists take over the government of the small Caribbean Island of Grenada, President Reagan orders the U.S. military to invade the island. After a brief battle, the communists are removed from office.

1983

Pop star Michael Jackson releases his album Thriller. It will go on to sell over 40 million copies.

1984

Representative Geraldine Ferraro of New York is chosen by Democratic presidential candidate Walter Mondale of Minnesota to run for vice president.

President Reagan easily defeats former vice president Walter Mondale to win re-election as president.

1986

The space shuttle Challenger explodes seventy-three seconds after lift-off, killing all seven crew members, including high school science teacher Christa McAulife, who had been chosen as the first civilian to travel into space.

After Ronald Reagan won election as president in 1980, relations with the Soviet Union worsened. Reagan launched a massive arms build-up. He replaced U.S. nuclear missiles in Western Europe faster than scheduled. He called the Soviet Union an "evil empire."

Reagan backed his tough talk with tough actions. In 1982, a group of Marxists took control of the tiny island of Grenada in the Caribbean Sea. (Communism grew out of the anti-capitalist teachings of Karl Marx, a German philosopher who inspired many rebels on the political left.) Reagan sent American troops to remove the Marxists. In El Salvador, Reagan gave aid to the government in its fight against Communist rebels. In Nicaragua, he helped pro-American contras fighting the Marxist Sandinista government. (In Spanish, contra means "against.")

What worried the Soviets most, though, was Reagan's plan for a new space-based defense system. Officially called the Strategic Defense Initiative (SDI), the plan was popularly called "Star Wars" after the science fiction movies. Reagan wanted a set of armed satellites that could orbit the earth and shoot down any nuclear missiles fired at the United States before they hit their targets. Many scientists warned that such a system would not work, but Reagan did not back down. To develop a similar system, the Soviets would have to spend billions of dollars. But the Soviet economy was failing and could not afford such a project.

In the middle 1980s, Mikhail Gorbachev became the new Soviet leader.

1986

Reports surface that the Reagan administration has sold weapons to the government of Iran in order to illegally support anti-government rebels in the Central American country of Nicaragua. After destroying evidence, administration officials deny the reports.

1987

The stock market falls by over 500 points in a single day, leading to the firing of 15,000 Wall Street workers.

President Reagan and Mikhail Gorbachev, the leader of the Soviet Union, agree to eliminate thousands of nuclear missiles.

1988

Vice President George Bush defeats Governor Michael Dukakis of Massachusetts in the presidential election.

1991

After the Middle Eastern nation of Iraq invades neighboring Kuwait, President Bush organizes Operation Desert Storm, in which United Nations troops, mostly from the United States, push Iraq out of Kuwait.

President Reagan and Mikhail Gorbachev
(Library of Congress)

He took his country in a new direction. Gorbachev and Reagan met several times and reached agreements limiting nuclear arms. In one 1987 deal, they agreed to eliminate thousands of nuclear missiles. The next year, Gorbachev announced that he was ending his country's bloody—and failing—war in Afghanistan. He also promised to pull Soviet troops out of Eastern Europe, where they had been since 1945. The Cold War was thawing.

Between 1989 and 1991, the Cold War ended. Unrest over communist rule had simmered in Eastern Europe for decades. People resented the lack of freedom and the hardships they had to suffer because state-run economies performed poorly. In 1989, thousands of frustrated people across Eastern Europe staged angry protests. They demanded change—and quickly got it. By late 1989, communist governments had fallen in Poland, Hungary, Czechoslovakia, and East Germany. Even the symbol of the Cold War, the Berlin Wall, was torn down.

1991

The Soviet Union collapses, breaking apart into a series of smaller independent republics. After Soviet leader Mikhail Gorbachev resigns, Boris Yeltsin becomes leader of Russia, the largest republic in the former Soviet Union.

1991

Computer scientists develop software that will later lead to the development of the World Wide Web (WWW).

1992

Although a video camera catches police beating African American motorist Rodney King, a jury finds the police innocent of any wrong-doing. After the decision is announced, riots spread throughout Los Angeles, starting in the African American community of South Central Los Angeles.

1992

Governor Bill Clinton of Arkansas defeats George Bush and Texas businessman Ross Perot in the presidential election.

Ben Nighthorse Campbell of Colorado becomes the first Native American elected to the Senate.

In 1991, communism fell in its original home, the Soviet Union. In a stunning series of events, the Soviet Union broke up. The first to leave were the former nations of Estonia, Latvia, and Lithuania, during a failed attempt to oust Gorbachev. Later, Russian Ukraine and Belarus declared the Soviet Union dead. Gorbachev resigned, and the Soviet Parliament disbanded. Most of the former Soviet republics joined a loose Commonwealth of Independent States (CIS). Russia—the largest of the former republics—remained an important country. It still had a large army and navy and huge stores of nuclear weapons. But it was weakened by political and economic problems. The new Russian government was no longer a rival, because it needed American and European aid.

After four decades, the Cold War was over. The United States and its allies were the winners. The United States was the world's strongest nation, the only remaining superpower.

Trouble in the Middle East

By 1991, the world seemed friendlier to the United States—at least in Europe. Trouble in the Middle East clouded America's future, however.

Large parts of the Mideast's huge Muslim population felt angry with the United States. They saw it as the symbol of Western culture and its many freedoms—social, economic, and political. That freedom threatened to over-whelm traditional Islamic culture, which strictly controlled people's private

1993
Six people die when Muslim terrorists explode a bomb in the parking garage underneath one of the two towers of New York City's World Trade Center.

1993
The North American Free Trade Agreement is signed, banning all trade barriers between the United States, Mexico, and Canada for fifteen years.

1994
In the midterm election, Republicans gain control of both the House of Representatives and the Senate for the first time since the 1950s

1995
Timothy McVeigh, a former soldier with a hatred of the U.S. government bombs a federal office building in Oklahoma City, Oklahoma, killing 168 men, women, and children.

lives, especially those of women.

Second, in its attempts to safeguard oil supplies and maintain stability, the United States had backed many undemocratic leaders who ruled with an iron hand and kept wealth in the hands of a few people. Two-thirds of the world's oil could be found in the Middle East. This made it vitally important to the economic well-being of many countries, especially the United States.

Finally, there was the issue of Israel. The creation of Israel as a home-land for Jews after World War II had forced tens of thousands of Palestinian Muslims from their homes. Even more became displaced when Israel occupied more land after wars in 1967 and 1974. Strong American support for Israel contributed to Muslim anger. That anger boiled over several times in the 1980s and 1990s.

The first Mideast trouble spot was Iran. In 1979, an uprising ousted the shah, or ruler, who had been a close American ally. This revolution put a strict, or fundamentalist, Muslim religious leader, the Ayatollah Ruhollah Khomeini, in control. When President Carter allowed the former shah to enter the United States, a group of Iranian students burst into the United States embassy and seized everyone there as hostages. Though some were released, the students continued to hold 53 American men.

Days became weeks, and weeks dragged into months. The students occasionally paraded the hostages—blindfolded and bound—in front of huge crowds of Iranians. "Death to America," they chanted. Carter tried diplo-

1996
President Clinton defeats Senator Robert Dole of Kansas to win reelection.

President Clinton agrees with Republicans to end the Aid to Families with Dependant Children welfare program, angering many of his supporters.

1999
The U.S. House of Representatives votes to impeach President Clinton for lying about an affair with a young White House intern. After holding hearings on whether to convict Clinton and remove him from office, the U.S. Senate votes not to convict him.

2000
Democratic presidential candidate Albert Gore of Tennessee chooses Joseph I. Lieberman, a U.S. senator from Connecticut, as his running mate. Lieberman becomes the first Jewish candidate nominated by a major political party to run for vice president.

2000
Although Vice President Albert Gore wins more votes than Texas governor George W. Bush in the presidential election, Bush wins more electoral votes when the U.S. Supreme Court votes 5-4 to halt a recount of disputed votes in Florida's returns.

Two U.S. Marines in Lebanon (National Archives)

macy and economic punishments to win the hostages' release. Nothing worked. In April 1980, he tried a military rescue. The attempt failed miserably. Photographs of the charred bodies of eight servicemen killed in a helicopter crash reminded many Americans of the failures in Vietnam. It took more than a year for Carter to negotiate the hostages' freedom. They left Iran the day that Ronald Reagan was sworn in to succeed him as president.

Reagan had his own Middle East troubles. In September 1983, he sent American troops to try to help restore order in Lebanon. That small country to Israel's north was torn by a civil war. A month later, a Muslim terrorist drove a truck loaded with dynamite into a U.S. Marine barracks in Lebanon, where it exploded. The blast killed 241 soldiers. Reagan vowed to keep American troops there. But those remaining were moved to the safety of American ships a few months later.

The next trouble spot was Iraq, Iran's neighbor. Iraq's dictator Saddam Hussein had fought a long and bloody war against Khomeini's Iran. That conflict had left Iraq deeply in debt and needing billions of dollars to rebuild. In August 1990, Saddam Hussein decided to do something to get the money he needed. He invaded Kuwait, a small neighbor with large oil reserves.

President George Bush—Reagan's two-term vice president who had been elected in 1988—declared "This aggression will not stand." He persuaded the United Nations Security Council to condemn the invasion and demand that Iraq pull out. Bush feared that Saddam's army would next invade Saudi Arabia. That country had the world's largest oil reserves but too small an army to resist Iraq. Bush persuaded Saudi Arabia to allow American troops on Saudi soil.

Over time, Bush forged a coalition of more than 30 countries. Some sent troops to help defend Saudi Arabia in Operation Desert Shield. Others provided money. The allied force—dominated by Americans—eventually numbered nearly 700,000 troops. Saddam refused to budge under diplomatic pressure. Late in 1990, the Security Council authorized using force to expel Iraq from Kuwait. In January 1991, the U.S. Congress gave Bush the go-ahead to send American troops into combat.

On January 16, Desert Shield became Operation Desert Storm. For six weeks, coalition planes bombed Iraq. On February 24, a ground attack began. Battered by intensive bombing, tens of thousands of Iraqi soldiers surrendered, and thousands more fled to Iran. The allied troops quickly liberated Kuwait—the war's objective. Some people suggested that Bush should overthrow Saddam. However, none of the Muslim allies would agree to such an action. Also, a growing number of critics said that the war was punishing both the military and civilians and should stop. After 100 hours of the ground war, Bush called a cease-fire on February 27.

Many Americans viewed the Gulf War as a tremendous victory. Most felt that the war had been just, like punishing a bully. It had proven the superiority of American military technology. Allied casualties had been minor—

President George Bush visiting troops during Operation Desert Storm, in 1991. (Library of Congress)

fewer than 200 troops died in the war. Some people felt that the Gulf War made up for a humiliating defeat in the Vietnam War (1964–1973). President Bush put the feeling into words: "The specter of Vietnam has been buried forever in the desert sands of the Arabian Peninsula."

The president's popularity surged. A poll showed that more than 90 percent of Americans approved his performance.

Although Kuwait was again free, Iraq continued to threaten world peace. Saddam was believed to be hiding biological, chemical, and possibly nuclear weapons. After President Bush announced a cease-fire, he agreed to allow UN inspectors to look for these weapons so that they might be destroyed. But Saddam cooperated only partly, and the inspectors left. In response, the United Nations banned Iraq from selling its oil until he followed through on his agreement.

Some critics charged that sanctions against oil sales hurt ordinary Iraqis more than their leader. When Saddam was allowed to sell some oil to buy food and medicine, he used the income for his own purposes, including rebuilding his army. As a result, thousands of Iraqis—including children—died of starvation and disease. Many Muslims blamed the United States.

American troops remained in Saudi Arabia. That country was home to Mecca and Medina, two of Islam's holiest sites. Many devout Muslims bitterly resented having American soldiers on sacred soil. Small groups of radical Muslims began to act on these feelings. They believed that any sacrifice they could make to help Islam succeed—even their lives—was worthwhile. Many had been hardened in the victorious struggle to push the Soviets out of Afghanistan. They were very dangerous.

In the 1990s, these groups launched several terrorist attacks against the United States. The first came in 1993, when a truck bomb exploded underneath one of two towers of New York City's World Trade Center. The damage was slight, and only five people died in the attack. The attack alarmed U.S. anti-terrorist experts, though. It was the first time foreign terrorists had attacked targets on American soil.

Three years later, a new threat emerged. A millionaire from Saudi Arabia named Osama bin Laden issued a startling declaration. Bin Laden called Muslims to join him in a campaign to punish Americans—civilians as well as soldiers. He declared "If Allah wills and I live, God willing I will expel the Jews and the Christians from Arabia." His first strike came in 1998. In August, two groups of bin Laden's agents drove trucks toward American embassies in two African cities. The massive bombs on the trucks exploded, killing hundreds of people and wounding thousands more. It was a sign of more deadly attacks to come.

America's Leaders

While these events played out on the world stage, Washington was torn by political bickering. All presidents in this period—Ronald Reagan, George Bush, and Bill Clinton—had troubles with Congress. All three also reflected the generally conservative shift in American public opinion. It no longer favored big government programs of the 1960s and 1970s.

Reagan took many steps to achieve his conservative goals. Besides slashing taxes, he reduced government regulation of business, saying it hurt the economy. He reduced government spending in many areas. Meanwhile, large-scale military budgets pushed up overall spending. Higher spending combined with deep tax cuts produced budget deficits—the federal government spent more money than it took in. To make up the difference, the government had to borrow money. As a result, the national debt began to soar. It climbed from $914 billion in 1980 to $1.8 trillion in 1985.

Reagan spoke movingly of freedom and patriotism. This made him very popular and to an extent protected him from criticism. This helped him when a scandal broke in his second term. It was revealed that members of Reagan's administration had sold weapons to Iran in an effort to improve relations with that country. They then used the money from the weapons sales to aid the rebels fighting the Marxist-leaning government of Nicaragua. (Nicaragua's leaders called themselves Sandinistas, after a rebel leader in the 1930s named Augusto Sandino.) That action violated a law passed by Congress that had banned aid to the contras. Congress held several investigations of what became known as the Iran-Contra scandal. One committee concluded that Reagan had abandoned his "moral and legal responsibility to take care that the laws be faithfully executed." Reagan's image was tarnished, but he recovered. When he left office in 1989, he was one of the most popular of all presidents.

Reagan also avoided blame for the economic impact of his deficit spending. During the 1980s, this spending had helped fuel economic growth. By the end of the decade, though, the mounting federal debt was $3.3 trillion, or $13,132 for every American. As president, George Bush had to face the consequences.

Huge sums of money were needed every year to pay interest on the money the government borrowed. These payments limited government spending in other areas. The limits became clear starting in 1990, when the economy went into a recession. The Gulf War pushed the debt even higher. Democrats in Congress wanted to pass new programs that would create jobs and help people out of the recession.

Bush, a conservative, had pledged not to raise taxes. He refused to go along with the Democrats because more spending would mean higher deficits. He and the Democrats argued back and forth about what to do. In the end, they did nothing. By 1992, most people were blaming the president for the economic hard times. Unfortunately for Bush, in 1992 he was running for re-election.

As the election neared, many Americans were fed up with the bickering between Republicans and Democrats that had plagued the Reagan and Bush years. Many lost interest in politics, but millions of Americans became deeply involved that year. They backed a third-party candidate. Billionaire H. Ross Perot. Perot won support because he was an outsider who criticized both Democrats and Republicans for "gridlocked government"—political maneuvering, like a traffic jam, that did nothing to solve problems. In the end, Perot won nearly 20 million votes, more than half the total amassed by President Bush.

The winner that year was the Democratic candidate, Arkansas governor William Jefferson Clinton, called Bill. Clinton was 47 years old—the first baby boomer to run for president. He had a probing mind and a powerful memory. More important, he was, like Reagan, an excellent speaker who related well to people. However, many people had nagging doubts about his character. Though some people had misgivings, he managed to persuade enough voters that he was more able to solve the nation's economic problems. Clinton won 44.9 million votes to Bush's 39.1 million, a margin narrower than Bush had won over Democratic Massachusetts Governor

Michael Dukakis four years earlier in 1988.

In some ways Bill Clinton was a traditional Democrat who wanted the government to get more involved in helping people. But his policies also showed the influence of the conservative movement that had been growing since the 1970s. He revealed this in his first inaugural address when he said, "It is time to break the bad habit of expecting something for nothing, from our government or from each other. Let us all take more responsibility, not only for ourselves and our families but for our communities and our country."

Clinton, like Reagan, was president for eight years. He was re-elected in 1996 in another three-way race against Republican Senator Robert Dole and Ross Perot, who ran again. Perot was less successful on the Reform ticket than in 1992.

Clinton took a conservative approach to fixing the nation's economy. He rejected massive public-works programs—the traditional Democratic approach. Instead, he stressed reducing the budget deficit. The strategy worked. Helped by other factors—including the computer and Internet revolution—the economy began to take off, beginning the long economic boom of the 1990s. By the end of the decade, the federal government even showed a surplus—it collected more than it spent.

Still, the wrangling between Republicans and Democrats in Washington continued throughout Clinton's eight-year presidency. Republicans blocked Clinton's efforts to name several people to high government posts. They passed laws he did not like, and he responded by vetoing them.

Republicans also pounced on stories of possible illegal actions by Clinton and his wife, Hillary Rodham Clinton, in a real-estate investment they had undertaken in Arkansas. A special prosecutor was named to investigate charges in what became known as Whitewater. Several of the Clintons' associates were convicted of felonies involving the failure of a savings and loan institution, but no criminal charges were brought against the president or his wife. (The Whitewater investigation closed after 18 months in 1996 at a cost of $52 million. The finding of no criminal charges was announced in September 2000, as Mrs. Clinton prepared to run, successfully, for the Senate.)

Bitter partisan feelings peaked in 1998 and 1999. Charges arose that Clinton had had an affair with a young White House intern, Monica

Lewinsky, and lied about it while under oath in a court proceeding. Republicans said that in doing so, Clinton had broken his oath of office to uphold the laws of the United States. After a lengthy investigation, the Republican-dominated House of Representatives voted to impeach the president. For only the second time in American history, a president was impeached. (Andrew Johnson was impeached in 1868, but not convicted by the Senate, and Richard Nixon had resigned in 1974, avoiding impeachment.)

The Constitution requires that the Senate must convict an impeached president to remove him from office. Early in 1999, the Senate put Clinton on trial. After weeks of legal arguments, the senators voted. Sixty-seven votes—two-thirds of the Senate—were needed to convict him of the charge and remove him from office. He was found not guilty on one charge. The vote was 50-50 on the other. Clinton continued as president.

Many Americans felt the Republicans were out to get Clinton—though many of the same people strongly disapproved of Clinton's behavior. While he remained in office, the Lewinsky scandal had an impact on the 2000 presidential campaign. Clinton's vice president, Al Gore, ran for the Democrats, but he could not shake the tarnish that Clinton's actions had left on the administration.

Despite the great economic success of the 1990s and despite winning the popular vote 51 million to 50.4 million, Gore did not win the election. He lost to the son of the man Clinton and Gore had defeated in 1992. George W. Bush won by a vote of 266 to 271 in the Electoral College, where votes are cast by electors equal in number to the senators and representative of each state. While promising to continue conservative economic policies, the second President Bush pledged to restore honor to the White House.

A Changing Country

Beneath these international changes and political tussles, the makeup of the American people changed. Some of the changes continued earlier trends. Some were new.

In earlier decades, the population had started to shift away from the Northeast and North Central states toward the South and West. This trend continued throughout the 1980s and 1990s. Three of the country's five most populous states—California, Texas, and Florida—came from this area, called the Sunbelt for its warmer weather. Fourteen of the 25 largest cities were in the South and West as well.

Though these cities were growing, more Americans were moving to the suburbs outside of cities. In fact, by 2000 more than half of all Americans lived in suburbs. The growth of suburbs helped change the character of American life. More people lived in single-family homes than in apartment buildings or townhouses, as had been the case when cities were more prominent. Many suburbs had no public transportation, increasing Americans' reliance on cars. And many suburbs had no commercial center like the old city downtown district. Instead, people drove to malls to do their shopping.

Another important change was the rising number of older people compared to young people. Families were having fewer children. People were also living longer. The average life expectancy reached 74 for men and 77 for women by the end of the century. This trend had important consequences on American life. The growing number of older Americans—many of whom needed medical

The Shifting American Population

During the second half of the twentieth century, many Americans moved from the Northeast and Midwest to the South and West.

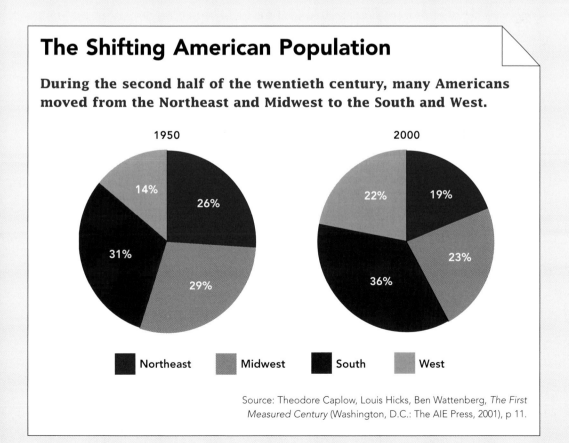

Source: Theodore Caplow, Louis Hicks, Ben Wattenberg, *The First Measured Century* (Washington, D.C.: The AIE Press, 2001), p 11.

care—contributed to the growth of health care spending. Many families had to find ways to care for elderly parents and grandparents who could no longer care for themselves. Also, the growing number of people collecting social security checks was an important policy issue because fewer workers were paying into the system as the government was sending more money out.

The American population changed in another way. New immigration laws made it easier for people to enter the United States than it had been since early in the century. The growing American economy contrasted with economic and political troubles in other lands led millions of people to come to the United States. The result was a boom in immigration. From 1960 to 1980, just fewer than 8 million people came to the United States from other lands. From 1980 to the late 1990s, that number jumped to more than 14 million.

These new immigrants also brought a new flavor to American life. The vast majority—nearly 12 of the 14 million—came from Asian countries, such as the Philippines, China, and India, and Latin American countries, such as Mexico, Cuba, and the Dominican Republic. The Latino population of the United States boomed in this period. In 1980, only 6.4 percent of the population was Latino. By the 2000 census, the proportion had almost doubled. Latinos outnumbered African Americans and had become the single largest ethnic minority in the United States.

Another change was the fragmentation (splitting up into smaller groups) of American society. The 1960s had launched a movement of ethnic pride. While many agreed that the contributions of different ethnic groups were to be treasured, some worried that the emphasis on separateness signaled a pulling away from common ground, from American-ness. The breaking up of American society into small groups could be seen in other ways as well. Radio stations began to play music targeted at specific groups rather than larger audiences. Magazines, too, aimed to reach narrow audiences—older people, hunting enthusiasts, computer gamers, and so on. And in the age of cable television, even TV networks focused in target audiences, such as those interested in cooking, home repair, science fiction, or old-time TV shows.

Some experts said that Americans were becoming isolated from each other. Others said that the opposite was happening. New technology, they said, was making the United States an interconnected nation.

During the 1990s, computers and the Internet changed the way Americans communicate. (CORBIS)

Two of the most dramatic forms of new technology involved computers. One of them was electronic mail, or e-mail, and the other was the Internet. Although this means of communicating over computers had existed since the late 1960s, it had only been used in select government and university laboratories. However, beginning the early 1980s, computer technology had advanced enough to allow computers to fit on a desktop. By the end of the 1980s, millions of Americans had computers in their own homes.

In 1991, computer scientists designed computer software programs that led to what is called the World Wide Web (WWW), or Web, for short. Two years later, software known as MOSAIC (later renamed Netscape) gave users a graphical interface, or visual means of viewing text and pictures on the Internet. Combined with electronic mail—text (and more recently sound and picture) messages that can be sent between computers anywhere in the world), the Internet forever changed the way Americans and people worldwide communicate with each other.

Other kinds of technology, such as facsimile (fax) machines and portable cellular phones, also helped kept people in constant touch. Web sites, radio phone-in shows, and TV town meetings give people more chances to speak their minds. Those who said that Americans were more connected than ever also pointed to increases in volunteering by Americans who used some of their time to improve the lives of others. Americans were just as dedicated as ever to having a strong, vibrant country, they said.

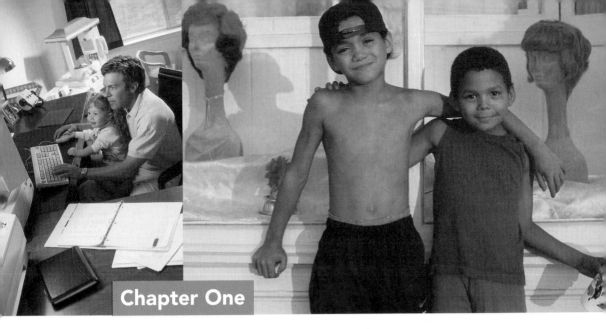

Chapter One

Family Life

The American family changed greatly during the twentieth century. At its end, families were smaller, with fewer children, and much more likely to live in a city or suburb than in 1920.

The twentieth century was marked by declining birth rates and increased life expectancy. By 2000, the United States had proportionately fewer children and more old people. In the late 1990s, 35 percent of the population was under 25 years old, and 12 percent was over 65. In 1900, more than half of all Americans had been under 25, and 4 percent were over 65.

Other trends that had begun early in the century gained momentum over time. The divorce rate, for example, had risen in fits and starts throughout the century. It doubled between 1900 and 1960, when it reached nine per thousand married couples. In 1975, it shot up to twenty divorces per thousand married couples. This was largely a result of "no-fault" divorce laws. Many states passed these laws that allowed people to divorce without blaming one partner. After that, the divorce rate remained high. It was estimated that four out of ten couples who married in 2000 would get divorced.

Americans continued to move. Now their mobility was eased by jet airplanes that cut travel time and recreational vehicles that allowed families to live comfortably on the road. Only 62 percent of Americans lived in the state where they were born, compared to 79 in 1900.

With the birthrate declining, most population growth came from newcomers. Immigration, which had been high at the beginning of the century, was greatly restricted between 1924 and 1965. In 1965, new laws lifted these restrictions. Immigrant families arrived in high numbers from the Western Hemisphere, Asia and sub-Saharan Africa, bringing with them new languages, religions, and family customs.

The New Family

By now, even people's definition of what made a family had changed. In a 1989 poll sponsored by the Massachusetts Mutual Insurance Company, three-quarters of the people rejected traditional definitions based on two parents and their children living together. Instead, they defined a family as "a group of people who love and care for one another." This changing attitude was reflected in American society, where families were extremely varied.

Ten times more adults lived alone in 1990 than had in 1900. Though most people still married, more couples chose not to have children. Many more marriages ended in divorce, leaving many families headed by a single parent. Some parents never married, and the stigma attached to children born "out of wedlock" had almost disappeared. There were blended families, formed when two single parents remarried and together raised children from earlier marriages. There were families in which the partners were homosexuals. There were also more marriages between partners of different races.

The physical surroundings of families had changed as well. In 1900, 60 percent of all Americans lived in rural areas. By the end of the century, 75 percent lived in cities and suburbs. Homes had changed, too. The average single-family home built toward the end of the century had at least two stories, three bedrooms, two and a half bathrooms and a garage. It was much bigger than houses built in the boom that followed World War II (1941–1945). At the same time, more people lived in multi-family housing—apartment buildings and townhouses attached to others like them.

Technology and Daily Life

Technology had helped to change American family life. Homes were more comfortable than ever. Ninety-three percent had central heating in 1997, compared to 50 percent in 1950. Even more remarkable, 78 percent of homes were air-conditioned, a luxury afforded by less than 1 percent in 1950.

Compared to mid-century, more homes had refrigerators and automatic clothes washers. The spread of dishwashers, garbage disposals, clothes dryers, and microwave ovens reduced the amount of housework. Women still did most of that work—even when both parents worked outside the home. One study found that working mothers spent eighteen hours a week on housework but working fathers only three. Nevertheless, housework was considerably less burdensome than the fifty to sixty hours required in the 1920s and 1930s.

Compared with nineteenth-century families, modern families had more time to be together. People worked fewer hours each day and fewer days each week than earlier in the century. Workers had more holidays and more paid vacation time as well. One long-term study of a Midwestern city found that fathers and mothers both spent more time with their children in 1999 than they had in 1924. Experts found it noteworthy because more mothers now worked, and the school day had grown longer.

Nevertheless, families often complained about the lack of time together. Parents spoke of making the time they had meaningful—"quality time." Moving to the suburbs extended the time needed to travel to and from work. Automobiles that had given Americans so much mobility were often stuck in huge traffic jams.

Wherever they lived, families enjoyed a dazzling variety of entertainment technology. In the early 1900s, a family might gather in the evening to read together or play games. A few well-to-do families might listen to music on a Victrola or the piano. By the end of the century, family members could pass the time with various electronic devices. These included television, video recorders, compact disk players, computers, and game players. Often, each person chose a different kind of entertainment, and the family split into different parts of the home.

Family Pressures

Despite modern advances, American families felt many pressures. Family income had nearly doubled between 1950 and 1970. From then until the late 1990s, though, it increased only 16 percent.

That slow rate of increase was one reason that more than 60 percent of all married women worked. Many families needed two incomes to get by.

Single mothers struggled even more. If they worked, many had low-paying jobs and did not receive regular child support.

As many factories moved to nations where labor costs were lower, the drop in manufacturing jobs hit the middle-class hard. Many workers took jobs in stores, hotels, and restaurants which paid far less than factories. Betty Lizana saw the Mississippi factory where she had worked close down, forcing its workers to scramble for new jobs. "There is no manufacturing any more," she said. "It seems like the only people who advertise are K-Mart. But sometimes those are part-time jobs and they don't pay much, either."

Social pressures hit families as well. The sharp increase in the number of older Americans changed family life. Parents caring for both children and aging parents were called the "sandwich generation" because they were caught between two sets of needs.

The rising number of divorces meant more families had to face the wrenching problems of breaking up. Some families con-

Sarah Brown, a single mother from Rochester, New York, received government assistance to help support her and her child while she worked in a machine shop. (© David H. Wells/CORBIS)

fronted issues such as physical abuse, drug addiction, and alcoholism. Many others simply wrestled with the day-to-day challenge of balancing work and family life.

Children

Economic pressures brought about a major change in child rearing. By 1980, the majority of married women with children under six years old worked outside the home. As a result, eight to nine million children were placed in some kind of day care every day.

A small number of parents were lucky to have day-care centers at the workplace, set up and paid for by their employers. Others relied on family members or neighbors, who watched the children in their own homes. Many parents placed their children in a growing number of commercial day-care centers. By the early 1990s, child care was an $8 billion business.

Many parents worried about the impact of these arrangements on their children. A report by the Families and Work Institute in New York City reinforced their concerns. It concluded: "More than one-third [of children in day care] are in situations that can be detrimental to their development. Most of the rest are in settings where minimal learning is taking place." The study provided some reassurance, though. It pointed out that "high quality care can enhance a child's development." That still left many parents worried about making sure their children's day care was "high quality." Congress continued to reject proposals to fund day care.

Another concern was "latchkey children." This term referred to children who returned from school to an empty house because parents were at work. Some mothers worked part-time so they could be home when their children arrived after school. Other mothers and fathers worked at different times—one during the day and one at night—so one parent could always be at home. Some relied on older children or a relative to care for younger ones. Local communities also tried to help. Many schools and public libraries offered after-school programs. Concerned about children's safety, many communities gave children special phone numbers they could call in an emergency.

Teens

Many of those latchkey children were teenagers, who were often portrayed negatively in the media throughout the century's last decades.

Critics spoke of disturbingly high levels of sexual activity, sexually transmitted diseases, drug and alcohol use, suicide, and smoking. Highly publicized shootings at several schools led many to say that video games and movies had made teens insensitive to violence. Meanwhile, public health officials pointed to studies showing that more than 20 percent of teens were overweight.

During Ronald Reagan's two terms as president, First Lady Nancy Reagan launched a highly publicized campaign aimed at instilling moral behavior in America's youth. She urged them to "just say no"—to sex, drugs, alcohol, and cigarettes. Conservatives applauded this approach, but many analysts called the campaign simplistic. They said smoking, drinking, and drug use were symptoms of underlying social and personal problems. They urged family counseling and more spending on treatment programs.

Many school systems made Mrs. Reagan's call for abstinence the theme of drug and sex education programs. Thousands of

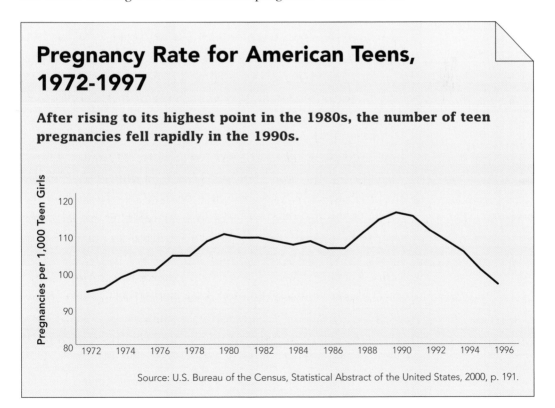

Pregnancy Rate for American Teens, 1972-1997

After rising to its highest point in the 1980s, the number of teen pregnancies fell rapidly in the 1990s.

Source: U.S. Bureau of the Census, Statistical Abstract of the United States, 2000, p. 191.

teens pledged abstinence from sex, drugs, alcohol, and tobacco. The group Students Against Destructive Decisions (SADD, earlier called Students Against Drunk Driving) promoted positive behaviors. At the same time, treatment centers grew across the country providing help for teens who had fallen into the trap of addictive behaviors.

Underneath the media alarms, though, research results about America's teens were quite positive. Teen smoking dropped nearly in half between 1985 and 1999. A University of Michigan study showed that by the late 1990s drug use among teens had leveled off. It was, in fact, lower than it had been in 1979—though alcohol use remained high. The rate of teen pregnancies, after peaking in 1990, dropped steadily every year. By 1997, it was below the 1972 level.

Most revealing, perhaps, were teens' views of their own lives. In a Department of Education poll, 76 percent of teens said they felt pressure to make good grades and to get into college. Only 32 percent felt pressure to use drugs or be sexually active.

Volunteerism showed another positive side to teen life. More than thirteen million teens volunteered to help friends, neighbors, and even strangers in community service programs each year. One study showed that about 60 percent of all teens did some kind of volunteer work, giving as much as three and a half hours a week of their time. They did a wide range of tasks, from tutoring younger children to working on community clean-up efforts to helping the homeless. The Independent Sector, a source of information on nonprofit work, valued teen volunteer work at more than $34 billion—a substantial contribution to American society.

Still, there was clearly tension between the generations. Another study found that most adults saw teens in negative ways.

The Elderly

For many decades, old age had meant weakness and debility. By century's end, though, most sixty- and seventy-year-olds were relatively healthy, active, involved adults. Many could retire in financial comfort. They used their free time to pursue hobbies, work in the community, and travel. Some social analysts began to split the elderly into two groups—the active "young old" and the more frail "oldest old."

A growing number of Americans moved into nursing homes as they reached retirement age. (Archive Photos)

Many in the second group—people over eighty-five—suffered from serious physical and mental problems. Many lived in nursing homes, where some experienced neglect and even abuse. Since these facilities could be very expensive, many others lived with their adult children. Even some retirees found themselves caring for their own aged parents. As one commented, "I want to enjoy my grandchildren; I never expected that when I was a grandparent I'd have to look after my own parents."

Many older Americans joined the American Association of Retired Persons (later simply shortened to AARP, or "arp"). Formed in 1958, this association grew to include more than thirty million members by the late 1990s. AARP offered members discounts at many stores and travel services. Most important, perhaps, AARP was a powerful lobby in Washington, D.C. Older Americans tended to vote at a higher percentage than any other group. AARP used that fact to push Congress to pass laws that favored older people.

Still, even AARP could not win one of its major goals. A big problem facing the elderly was the rising cost of prescription drugs. The federal government helped fund older people's health care costs through the Medicare program. However, Medicare did not cover medicines prescribed by doctors. AARP wanted to add this benefit to Medicare. The growing number of old people and sharply rising prescription prices worried many in Congress, though. No bill was passed during the twentieth century.

Promoting Family Values

The rise of conservative politics, symbolized by the 1980 election of Republican President Reagan, led to renewed focus on American families.

Conservatives championed "family values." They attacked teen pregnancy, birth control, illegal drug use, homosexual living arrangements, and many other behaviors that they saw as undermining the family. In the early 1990s, a TV sitcom featured an unmarried single character, Murphy Brown, who decided to have a baby. Vice President Dan Quayle denounced the plot line as glorified immorality. Critics charged Quayle with attempting to censor television.

Democrats took a different approach. They talked about helping families to balance the responsibilities of work and home life. They proposed making it easier for working people to cope with family emergencies. In 1993, they finally succeeded in turning the Family and Medical Leave Act into law. This law required employers to give workers time off to care for newborns or sick family members.

Another sign of the growing family values debate was the growth of the home school movement. By the late 1990s, nearly 900,000 students were being taught by their parents in their own homes. The reasons varied. Many parents complained that public schools were unsafe, overcrowded, and had ineffective educators. A large percentage of home schoolers were fundamentalist Christians. They complained that schools were teaching "secular humanism"—a watered-down morality that ignored the teachings of the Bible. Many fundamentalists objected to the teaching of human evolution in science classes.

Poor Families and Welfare Reform

Another family issue that received much attention in Washington was welfare. There were two main welfare programs in which the government helped poor families. The federal food stamp program provided coupons that recipients could use to buy food. Under the Aid to Families with Dependent Children (AFDC) program, about four million of the country's poorest single mothers received checks that could be used to support their families in any way they chose.

During the 1970s and 1980s, Republican conservatives attacked these programs. They charged that welfare payments created a culture of dependence in which poor people had no reason to find a job. They said that AFDC payments discouraged men from staying with their families because only single mothers—not married couples—received government checks. When he was president, Ronald Reagan sharply cut spending on food stamps, welfare, school lunches, and job training. Still, Republicans wanted to overhaul the system completely.

When he ran for president in 1992 , Democrat Bill Clinton appealed to middle-class taxpayers by calling for welfare reform. He promised to "change welfare as we know it." Republicans in Congress passed two welfare reform bills, but Clinton vetoed both as too harsh. By 1996, though, he was running for re-election. After getting the Republican Congress to pass a revised welfare-reform bill, he signed it. The new law put a two-year limit and a five-year lifetime cap on a person's ability to receive benefits. It also abandoned federal control of welfare payments and put the program in the hands of the states. This meant that each state could make its own rules.

Liberal Democrats protested strongly. New York Senator Daniel P. Moynihan called the new law "an obscene act" that abandoned nearly nine million children. But it was too late. Though many analysts predicted terrible consequences, widespread misery did not follow immediately. States were charged with developing programs to train people so they could get jobs. The timing was lucky—welfare reform took place in the middle of the 1990s economic boom. With the economy expanding, many former welfare recipients found work.

But the long-term effects of the law remained unclear. What would happen to former recipients when a recession hit? How would the children of newly employed mothers fare in day care and in school? And what would happen to women who had very little education, few job skills, or personal problems that made work difficult? How would they cope when they reached the five-year lifetime limit on benefits?

The Homeless Problem

Economic changes and government policies contributed to the rise of a new problem in America's cities—homelessness.

Cuts in welfare spending had already driven many families deeper into poverty. At the same time, housing costs were rising. Low-cost housing was harder to find. As a result, large numbers of people could not afford a place to live.

Analysts could not pinpoint the actual number of homeless people. By the late 1980s, there might have been 500,000 to 600,000 homeless individuals. About 60 percent of them were single, but the rest were in families. Around a fourth of all homeless people were children under 18. Up to a third of homeless adults had jobs. They just could not earn enough money to pay rent.

Cities and community groups tried to help the homeless in various ways. They set up soup kitchens to serve food and shelters to provide a place to sleep. By the later 1990s, some estimated that two million people were homeless. Such problems had existed during the Great Depression of the 1930s. It was more puzzling that modern homelessness existed alongside one of the nation's periods of greatest prosperity.

A political button calls for the end of homelessness.
(Private collection)

Family Health

Another difficult family issue was health care. Costs began to skyrocket in the 1970s. By 1980, the amount Americans spent on health had more than tripled to $247.3 million.

By 1990, heath care costs had reached $699.4 billion. Near the end of the decade, spending had soared to more than $1.1 trillion. The effect could be seen on personal spending. In 1970, people spent only 9 percent of their income on health care. By 1997, that figure was 17 percent.

The aging population and the rising cost of prescription drugs contributed to these climbing costs. Another factor was the fact that new ways of diagnosing and treating diseases were often quite expensive. New diseases added to the problem as well. AIDS (acquired immune deficiency syndrome) was identified early in the 1980s and spread very rapidly. At first, everyone who had AIDS died. A crash research program identified how the disease developed. Later work found medicines that could treat—

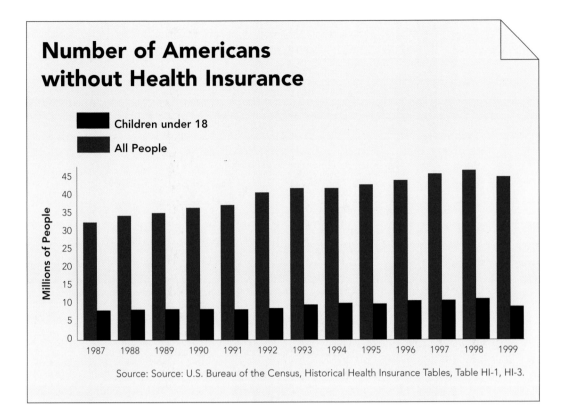

Number of Americans without Health Insurance

■ Children under 18

■ All People

Millions of People

45
40
35
30
25
20
15
10
5
0

1987 1988 1989 1990 1991 1992 1993 1994 1995 1996 1997 1998 1999

Source: Source: U.S. Bureau of the Census, Historical Health Insurance Tables, Table HI-1, HI-3.

though not cure—AIDS. But these drugs cost a great deal of money, as did the care of people with AIDS.

The rising costs caused major problems. Unlike other industrialized countries, the United States had no system of universal government-funded health care. The federal government did cover many health costs of the elderly and the poor under Medicare and Medicaid, respectively.

The vast majority of Americans, though, received health insurance from their employers. Employers contracted with insurance companies who paid doctors and hospitals.

The system had worked well until health care costs began to soar. Increased costs cut into insurance company profits and caused some to lose money. Insurance companies responded by dramatically raising prices for insurance premiums charged employers. These premium price hikes battered employers. They began to look for ways to hold down insurance costs. Some businesses joined health maintenance organizations (HMOs). These groups promised to hold down health care costs by focusing on preventive care—and by limiting peoples' treatment options. Other companies lowered premiums by cutting back on the benefits they offered employees. Some passed part of the cost on to their workers. Some simply dropped health insurance.

These changes had two results. First, many Americans were forced to spend more on health care. Second, the number of people who had no health insurance rose sharply almost every year from 1987 to 1999.

When he ran for president in 1992, Clinton promised to solve the health care crisis. He put his wife, Hillary Rodham Clinton, in charge of a group to find a solution. They settled on a complex program in which the federal government would provide health care coverage for all Americans. The plan was popular at first, but not for long. Republicans in Congress said it would result in higher taxes. Many businesses—especially insurance companies—mounted a campaign that convinced many Americans that the plan would not work. Eventually, President Clinton recognized that opposition was too strong to pass legislation. He withdrew the plan from Congress.

Still, Congress took some small steps. One new law made it possible for workers to continue their health insurance coverage if they changed jobs. Another created a program to provide health insurance for poor children. Both plans provided some help to targeted groups. Neither did anything to halt the rise in uninsured Americans—or the cost of health care.

The Men's Movements

In the1960s and 1970s, attention was focused on the changing role of women in society. Now many groups, especially conservative ones, focused on men.

In divorce decisions where children were involved, most judges ordered the father to make monthly payments to support his children. However, many fathers for many reasons skipped payments or never paid at all. Criticism of these "dead beat dads" became widespread in the media. Social policy makers grew concerned about the large number of single women raising their children in poverty. Many states passed aggressive laws to force payment of child support. At the same time, several movements rose to promote more responsible behavior among men.

In 1995, Nation of Islam leader Louis Farrakhan called for a "Million Man March" in Washington. He hoped to convince black men to play a stronger, more constructive role in the lives of their own and other African American children. Because Farrakhan had expressed extreme anti-white views, some black leaders refused to cooperate. Others criticized him for not including African American women in his campaign. Still others, however, decided that the issue was larger than these differences. The march was one of the largest ever held in Washington. There men were urged to take more responsibility for their families and their communities. "Every one of you must go back home and join some church, synagogue, temple or mosque," he told the crowd. "Join organizations that are working to uplift black people."

The Promise Keepers, founded in the early 1990s, stressed fundamental Christian beliefs. This predominantly white group staged rallies where tens of thousands of men gathered to listen to speeches and pray. In 1997, it held a rally in Washington, D.C. where several hundred thousand men participated.

The National Organization for Women (NOW), a feminist group, organized opposition to the Promise Keepers expressing concern about the group's belief in the biblical instruction that wives should submit to their husbands. NOW claimed that Promise Keepers were not advocating male responsibility but male control. The Promise Keepers denied those charges and continued its work.

A third—and very different—men's movement was launched by the poet Robert Bly. Bly used poetry and mythology to help men learn to express their feelings. He also advised that older, experienced males should mentor younger men. He and his followers held workshops across the country.

One thing was clear: by 2000 family policy was more political than ever before. Conservatives blamed liberals for being too lax about enforcing morality. Liberals blamed conservatives for forcing their values on others and violating family privacy. The family was more controversial than ever.

Chapter Two

Social and Political Attitudes

Ronald Reagan (Library of Congress); **Bill Clinton and his wife Hillary at the Democratic Convention in 1992.** (© STONE LES/CORBIS SYGMA)

Intense political feelings had marked the 1960s and 1970s. Tens of thousands turned out to protest the Vietnam War and to support civil rights and women's rights. The 1980s and 1990s had a different tone. People generally moved away from political activism. Many people focused on building their own lives.

Yet sixties' activism had left its mark. People had come to believe that ordinary people could change the world. Many joined local groups that worked to help children, older people, or the homeless. By the late 1990s, more than 100 million adults volunteered their time every year.

Actions by presidents Ronald Reagan, George Bush, and Bill Clinton promoted volunteerism, though in different ways. Budget cuts during the Reagan years meant that the government no longer supplied many social services. Many charity groups had to pick up this work, and they relied on volunteers to carry on their missions. Bush launched a foundation in 1990 to encourage more people to take part in volunteer work. Clinton formed AmeriCorps, inviting young people to undertake community service. In 1997 Clinton and three former presidents—Bush, Jimmy Carter, and Gerald Ford—joined to spearhead the creation

of a new organization, called "America's Promise." Its chief goal
was to recruit volunteers to help children. Retired general Colin
Powell led the group at first and worked tirelessly for its success.

The 1960s and 1970s had changed attitudes, too. Many
white Americans had accepted a basic goal of the Civil Rights
Movement—equal rights before the law. Many, too, had come to
reject long-held negative stereotypes about African Americans.
Fewer people thought women should stay in the home or that
women should be limited to only certain jobs.

People were more accepting of others' differences. African
American, Native American, and Latino cultures had gained
wider acceptance among other groups. There was a new surge of
interest in the ethnic backgrounds of Asian and European
Americans as well. People of widely different backgrounds
enjoyed food from other countries, such as Japan, India,
Ethiopia, and Cuba. The popularity gained by these flavors
became clear when salsa—the Latino dip—passed ketchup as the
nation's top-selling condiment.

Politics in America

While Americans had become more tolerant, many also grew
more conservative. Conservative thinkers and leaders gained followers by pushing three sets of ideas.

First, they wanted to make the federal government smaller
and put power in the hands of state and local leaders.
Conservatives argued that big government programs, like Lyndon
Johnson's "War on Poverty," had failed. They said that government spending was far too high. These ideas became popular in
part because many people mistrusted the government.
Washington officials had lied about the progress of the Vietnam
War. The Watergate scandal had revealed serious abuses of
power. These events had chipped away at people's faith in the
government.

The second set of ideas focused on the economy.
Conservative thinkers blamed the country's economic troubles on
high taxes. Families struggling to survive found their calls to cut
taxes very appealing. These thinkers also charged that the government rules aimed at ending pollution or protecting worker
safety had gone too far. These regulations made it too hard for
companies to do business and prevented the economy from grow-

ing. This argument appealed to businesspeople and to many workers who had lost their jobs.

The third set of ideas looked at culture. Conservatives blamed television, movies, and music for furthering immoral actions. Rising drug use and rising crime, they said, showed that Americans were abandoning God. Baptist preacher Jerry Falwell formed a group called the Moral Majority. The group protested abortion and giving equal rights to homosexuals. They called for laws that would have children say prayers every day in school.

Ronald Reagan brought these three sets of ideas together in his campaign for president in 1980. He won a landslide victory over Jimmy Carter. Many factors contributed to Reagan's win. Carter's failure to fix the economy or to rescue the American hostages held in Iran cost him many votes. Reagan had a sunny personality that made many Americans feel confident. But Reagan's conservative ideas also played a big role. Many Americans were tired of big government, high taxes, and a poor economy.

Conservative ideas remained powerful to the end of the century. Reagan was followed by his vice president, George Bush. He also backed many conservative goals. Even Bill Clinton, the Democrat who won election in 1992 and 1996, was conservative on some issues. Clinton backed many traditional Democratic causes, such as civil rights, women's rights, and support for unions. But he also supported conservative economic policies. He wanted to help businesses grow, thinking that would make the economy grow and create more jobs. He also changed the nation's welfare system, a major conservative goal.

Congress grew more conservative as well. Democrats—who tended to be liberal—had enjoyed majorities in one or both houses of Congress most years from the early 1930s to 1980. But Reagan's election victory in 1980 also swept Republicans into a majority in the Senate. They held that majority for most of the eighties and nineties. And in 1994, for the first time in more than 40 years, Republicans won a majority in the House of Representatives.

The 1994 House victory was the work of conservative Republican Newt Gingrich. He crafted that win with a clever strategy. First he wrote a set of goals called the "Contract With

America." The goals included several new laws the Republicans promised to pass if they won a majority in the House. These laws would limit government power, cut taxes, and help businesses. Then Gingrich got Republican candidates across the country to agree to support the contract.

When the Republicans did win a House majority, Gingrich became Speaker of the House—the leader of that part of Congress. He skillfully got the House to pass many of the promised new laws. But Democrats had more power in the Senate. Also, many Republicans there were more moderate than their House colleagues. In addition, Democratic president Bill Clinton was unwilling to accept some of the contract's ideas. As a result, few of Gingrich's ideas actually became law. Still, he and his conservative followers were major powers in Washington.

Changes in Crime

Rising crime rates in the 1970s and 1980s helped conservatives win support. Between 1960 and 1990, the number of all crimes tripled. The number of violent crime rose five times. Conservatives' promises to be tough on crime appealed to worried Americans.

Rising drug use helped fuel the growth in crime. Many drug

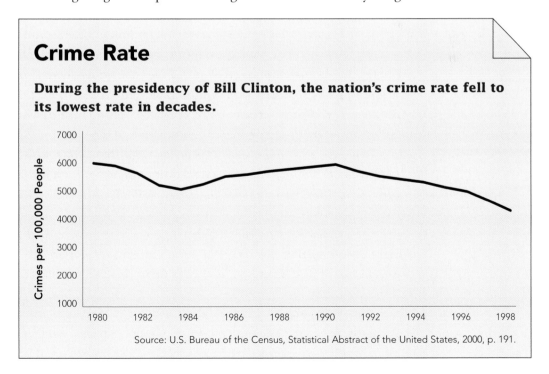

Crime Rate

During the presidency of Bill Clinton, the nation's crime rate fell to its lowest rate in decades.

Source: U.S. Bureau of the Census, Statistical Abstract of the United States, 2000, p. 191.

users committed crimes to get the money they needed for drugs. Rival gangs vied for control of drug sales in certain areas, leading to fights and shootings. Also, state and national governments passed tougher anti-drug laws, leading to more arrests.

As the chart on page 39 shows, the crime rate rose steadily from the early 1980s to 1991. Then it dropped from 1991 to 1992 and fell each year to the end of the decade.

Local officials hired more police officers. They also used police differently. More officers were sent to walk around neighborhoods instead of staying in their patrol cars. They built up better relations with the community and were in a better position to act when a crime was committed. New York City, under Mayor Rudolph Giuliani, led the way in this approach. And the city showed impressive results. In just five years in the 1990s, crime in New York dropped by an astounding 44 percent. Murders fell by 48 percent. This success prompted leaders in other cities to try the same methods.

Some analysts said that the growing economy of the 1990s helped lower crime rates, too. As people became better off, they committed fewer crimes.

The crime issue spurred two heated debates. One was over the death penalty. In 1976, the Supreme Court ruled that the Constitution did allow governments to execute people who were guilty of certain crimes. Soon after, thirty states passed death penalty laws. By 1999, nearly 700 people had been executed. Nearly 3,500 more were in prison under the death sentence. Supporters said that the death sentence was just. It punished the worst crimes with the worst possible penalty. They also said it prevented crime by stopping some people before they committed murder. Critics said there was little evidence of this effect. They also said that the death sentence was used far more against the poor, who could not afford skilled lawyers who could win them a better sentence.

The second debate was over gun control. Some people wanted to severely limit the sale of handguns. The National Rifle Association (NRA) opposed any such laws. The NRA said that the Second Amendment to the United States Constitution gave all citizens a fundamental right to own guns. The group had a great deal of influence in Washington. Still, Congress did pass two gun-control laws in the 1990s. One required people who wished to buy a handgun to wait five days. At that time, officials could check into the person's background for a criminal record. Another banned the sale of powerful guns such as those used by the military. Even these victories were not complete. The first law did not require the background check for guns sold at gun shows. The NRA convinced Congress not to pass another law to close that loophole.

Charlton Heston, president of the National Rifle Association, waves a rifle above his head during speech.
(© Houston Scott/CORBIS SYGMA)

While crime was falling, there were still many violent crimes. In 1999, the FBI reported more than 15,500 crimes in which a person was killed. While this was a drop from the peak of nearly 25,000 in 1991, it was still a lot of people. In several cases, one or two people with guns killed several people at a time. In some cases, teens or even younger children shot children and teachers at their schools. One series of connected crimes involved bombs. Starting in the late 1970s, three people had been killed and more than twenty injured when they received packages filled with a homemade bomb. The attacker—called the Unabomber—remained unknown for years. Finally, the bomber was allowed to publish a lengthy explanation of his actions in the *Washington Post*. A reader connected the ideas with some things his brother had said and contacted the police. They arrested the brother, a loner named Theodore Kaczynski. In 1998, Kaczynski pleaded guilty to some of the bombings and was sentenced to life in prison.

A New Threat

The shootings and the Unabomber case were disturbing enough. But in the 1990s a new threat appeared—terrorist attacks aimed at mass murder. The first attack came in New York in 1993. A group of Muslim extremists parked a car full of explosives in an underground garage at one of the two World Trade Center towers in New York City. The explosion killed six people and left more than 1,000 hurt. Several people were convicted for this attack and sentenced to life in prison. They included one of the group's leaders, Ramzi Yousef.

Two years later, a huge bomb destroyed the front of a federal office building in Oklahoma City. The blast killed 168 people and injured hundreds more. This time, the bomber turned out to be an American. Timothy McVeigh, a veteran of the armed forces, believed that the growing power of the government threatened freedom. McVeigh was found guilty of murder and executed. A man who had helped him was put in prison for his role.

In 1996, Atlanta hosted the Summer Olympic Games. One night during the games, a bomb exploded during a concert in a park. The blast killed one person and injured more than 100. The FBI identified a suspect—like McVeigh, a white American—but were unable to catch him.

Then in 1998, Islamic terrorists attacked again. On August 7, two truck bombs exploded outside two American embassies in Africa. The powerful explosions killed nearly 300 people and left hundreds of others hurt. Officials quickly identified a wealthy Saudi Arabian named Osama bin Laden as the culprit. Bin Laden resented the fact that American troops were stationed in Saudi Arabia, which had the two holiest cities of Islam. He also opposed American policy, which he said was too easy on Israel and too harsh against Muslims. He helped form a terrorist group named Al Qaeda. The group had training camps in several countries. It also placed small clumps of terrorists in dozens of countries. In a 1998 interview with ABC News, bin Laden said that he saw no difference between killing civilians or members of the armed forces.

In late 1999, the government stopped an attack before it could happen. Americans were planning to celebrate the ending of one millennium, or thousand-year period, and the beginning of another. Officials believed that Al Qaeda would stage an attack during these celebrations. On December 14, 1999, a man named Ahmed Ressam was arrested as he tried to enter the United States. Ressam's car had 130 pounds of explosives. He planned to attack the Los Angeles International Airport—one of the world's busiest.

Civil Rights

There were some important achievements in the area of civil rights. In 1990, Congress passed and George Bush signed into law the Americans with Disabilities Act. The law helped people with disabilities, such as those who could not see or hear or had to use a wheelchair. Such disabilities affected more than 40 million people. Under the law, barriers had to be removed to make life easier for them. For instance, where steps led to the entrance of a building, a ramp had to be added for people in wheelchairs. The law also stopped employers from discriminating against people with disabilities. Discrimination is any action that unfairly affects people of a particular group.

President Bush also signed a bill that kept the Voting Rights Act in effect. This law protected the rights of members of minority groups to vote. And he signed a new Civil Rights Act. This made it easier for workers to sue their employers for unfair actions taken against them because of their sex or race.

There was still a divide in how whites and people of color saw life in America. Most whites believed that prejudice, or unfavorable attitudes, and discrimination were largely in the past. People of color knew otherwise. As Richard Delgado, a legal scholar noted, "White people rarely see acts of blatant or subtle racism, while minority people experience them all the time." For example, police were more likely to stop and search cars driven by minorities than whites. In stores, they were more likely than whites to be watched closely. This practice came to be known as racial profiling.

African Americans especially suffered from discrimination. True, they had made great strides. Many blacks had gained economic success. Many held high political office or were important

President Goerge Bush signing the Americans with Disabilities Act in 1990. (National Archives)

figures in business, education, and culture. But, as the National Academy of Science concluded, "The status of black Americans today can be characterized as a glass that is half full—if measured by progress since 1939—or as a glass that is half empty—if measured by the persisting disparities between black and white Americans since the early 1970s." A higher percentage of blacks than whites lived in poverty. Unemployment was consistently higher among blacks. A higher proportion of blacks were in prison.

The situation grew dangerous in the nation's cities. There, large numbers of poor blacks lived in conditions that were becoming worse. Anger boiled over into violence several times. The worst incident took place in Los Angeles in 1992. That spring, four white police officers were tried for policy brutality when they had beaten a black motorist, Rodney King, the year before. The case was well-known because someone had video-taped the beating. But then an all-white jury found the four police officers not guilty. Many blacks in Los Angeles were enraged. Some took their rage to the street, and a riot began. Angry mobs destroyed stores and cars, and fires raged in the city for five days. More than fifty people died. About a billion dollars worth of property was damaged.

There were also some terrible outbreaks of white violence against blacks. Several African American churches in the South were burned. In 1998, three white men in Jasper, Texas, brutally murdered an African American man, James Byrd, Jr. But the Byrd case also revealed that the nation had progressed in race relations. Earlier in the century, when whites killed blacks they often went unpunished. The three killers of James Byrd were all found guilty of their horrible crime. Two were sentenced to death and the third to life in prison.

Some violent attacks were directed at homosexuals, or gays. The most vicious was the 1998 murder of a young man named Matthew Shepard. This murder prompted President Clinton to urge that gays should be added to a federal law against hate crimes. These are violent crimes committed against people because they belong to a particular group. Congress did not expand the law, however.

Another group that suffered from prejudice and discrimination was people who had AIDS (acquired immune deficiency syndrome). The disease first appeared in the early 1980s among homosexuals. At first, everyone who got the disease died. Some "straight," or heterosexual, Americans viewed the situation harshly. They thought that AIDS was a fitting punishment for the life that gays led, which they considered immoral. Because of this, the government was slow to devote funds to AIDS research.

Over time, though, attitudes changed. Some cases that received a lot of media attention softened people's views. A boy named Ryan White accidentally was given AIDS when he received some blood for medical reasons. His courage and dignity gave many Americans more sympathy with AIDS patients. Popular heterosexual basketball star Ervin "Magic" Johnson was another. He was forced to retire because he had the virus that causes AIDS. A powerful motion picture named *Philadelphia* helped change attitudes about AIDS and about homosexuals, too. It presented the AIDS issue in terms of the rights of the person with the disease. As more people from every group in society contracted AIDS, it became harder to judge them harshly. (See Chapter 7 for a discussion of efforts to find the causes of and treatments for AIDS.)

Ryan White
(Courtesy of the Ryan White Foundation)

Women's Rights

Women made many advances in the 1980s and 1900s. Several women reached high positions in government. Sandra Day O'Connor became the first woman to serve on the U.S. Supreme Court. Ruth Bader Ginsburg joined her twelve years later. Several women held Cabinet seats under presidents Reagan and Bush. In the Clinton administration women held two of the most powerful posts. Janet Reno served as Attorney General, and Madeleine Albright as Secretary of State. In 1984, Democratic presidential candidate Walter Mondale picked Geraldine Ferraro of New York as his running mate. Although they lost the election, Ferraro was the first woman on a major party's presidential ticket. Other women won election to many state offices across the country. In Washington State, women held more than 40 percent of the seats in the state legislature. In Arizona, women occupied the top five state offices, including governor and lieutenant governor.

Sandra Day O'Connor
(Library of Congress)

Women even succeeded in the male-dominated world of sports. By 1998, women made up one-third of all professional

Janet Reno
(Library of Congress)

athletes. Driving that success was Title IX, part of an education bill that Congress had passed back in 1972. Title IX required high schools and colleges to give women equal educational opportunities. Schools had to give women's sports as much funding as male sports. The result was a boom in the number of girls and young women who became athletes.

Women succeeded in business, too. By the late 1990s, they held more than 45 percent of all executive, administrative, and managerial jobs. Women headed up several major corporations. They had even narrowed the "gender gap"—the difference in earnings between men and women. Back in 1960, women had earned less than 61 cents for every 1 dollar a man earned. By the late 1990s, they were up to 73 cents.

Still, a wide 27-cent difference remained. And women also had problems gaining full acceptance. Many women said their careers were stopped by a barrier—a "glass ceiling." This barrier blocked them from reaching the highest positions in corporations or in their professions. While there had been progress, women were not yet equal to men.

Controversies

Three rights issues caused bitter fights. One was the Equal Rights Amendment (ERA). This would amend, or change, the Constitution. It stated that "equality of rights under the law shall not be denied or abridged . . . on account of sex." Congress passed the ERA in 1972. Within a year, the legislatures of 30 states ratified, or approved, the amendment. But eight more were needed before the ERA could officially be added to the Constitution.

Many women favored the ERA. They said it helped women's struggle for equality at school and at work. Phyllis Schlafly, a conservative activist, said the ERA would hurt not help women. She argued that with the ERA, women would be forced into the army. She said that women would have to work even if they did not want to because they would be responsible for half of a family's income. She organized and led a skillful fight against the ERA.

The debate over abortion stirred strong feelings as well. In the early 1970s, the Supreme Court had ruled that women had the right to have abortions. In this procedure, a woman's pregnancy is deliberately ended. As a result, the fetus, or developing baby, will not be born. Conservatives saw abortion as killing. They said

Over 300,000 abortion rights supporters attended a rally in Washington, DC in 1989. (© Susan Steinkamp/CORBIS)

that a person's life began the instant that the first cell that would become a baby was formed. They called themselves "pro-life." Supporters of abortion rights said women should be able to choose whether or not to continue a pregnancy. They called themselves "pro-choice." They said that if abortion were made illegal again, women would die. Women would still seek abortions, they said. But since the procedures would be against the law, they would be unsafe.

The Supreme Court struck down some state laws that put limits on abortion rights. But two decisions in the early 1990s did allow some restrictions. In both cases, only one vote kept abortions legal. That vote was cast by Sandra Day O'Connor, then the only woman justice on the Court. Since the Court was so closely divided, its makeup became a crucial battleground. Pro-life backers wanted the Court to have more conservatives, who would make abortions illegal. In the 1980s and 1990s, justices were named seven times. Each time, groups from both sides pushed senators to vote for or against the person depending on his or her views on abortion.

The two sides grew farther apart. The pro-choice people staged a big march on Washington, D.C., in 1989. About 300,000 called for maintaining the right to abortion. Most pro-life supporters also used marches and letter-writing campaigns to push their position. Some extremists, though, used violence.

The third issue that divided people was affirmative action. This policy aimed at helping women and members of minority groups overcome the effects of discrimination against them in the past. It targeted mainly African Americans, Latinos, and women. For many decades, these people had fewer chances to get a better education, better jobs, or more pay.

While many agreed with the goal, how to make it happen became highly controversial. Opponents argued that affirmative action would mean quotas. Employers, they said, would be forced to hire a certain number of women and minorities to avoid breaking the law. This might lead to hiring unqualified people and overlook white males who were better able to do the job. Opponents coined the term "reverse discrimination" to refer to this result. They said it was unfair. A 1978 Supreme Court decision (*Bakke v. University of California*) seemed to accept this position. The court ruled that universities could use race as one factor in deciding who to admit into medical school. It could not, though, set aside a specific number of places in the medical school for minority students.

Several more cases reached the Supreme Court. In one ruling, the justices said that such programs are valid only when there is strong evidence of widespread discrimination. In another, the justices said that affirmative action could be allowed, but programs had to be "narrowly tailored." In the late 1990s, voters in two states approved new laws about affirmative action. One was California, which had the most people of any state. Its law banned discrimination against anyone on the basis of sex, race, color, or ethnic origin in hiring and in college admissions. But the law also banned using preferences for women or minorities when making hiring or college admissions decisions. Clearly, the debate over affirmative action would continue into the new century.

Chapter Three

Education

In the last two decades of the twentieth century, education took on heightened importance. A major reason was changes in the workplace. Growing numbers of jobs called for workers to use computers and other new technologies. Expanding jobs in health care and engineering raised the demand for workers who could understand complex ideas. As a result, more than ever before, people needed a college education to get a job.

In the 1980s and 1990s, the number of students in college skyrocketed. Nearly half of all high school graduates were graduating from college four years later. In 1960, only 365,000 students graduated from college. By the late 1990s, the number had increased nearly four times, reaching more than 1.2 million a year. Larger numbers than ever before were taking their schooling even further. In 1999, more than 400,000 people earned master's degrees. Nearly 46,000 more received doctorates. This was more than four times the number of people getting those degrees back in 1960.

Meanwhile, many new technologies became a vital part of education itself. Teachers from first grade to twelfth grade began to use computers. By 1999, schools had more than 10 million computers, enough to have one for every five students. And teachers used the Internet to reach outside the classroom. Nearly two-thirds of all classrooms across the country had computers

Graduation Day (LEFT) **at the University of Miami, in 1999** (© Tony Arruza/CORBIS); **a preschool class** (RIGHT) **in Aberdeen, Washington, in 1989.** (© Matthew McVay/ CORBIS)

that could tap into the Internet. New inventions improved on older tools. Videos replaced movies, making it easier to show educational programs. Then laserdiscs and CD-ROMs came along and replaced videos. These devices stored huge amounts of information. More important, they allowed teachers to instantly reach any bit of that information rather than having to waste time fast-forwarding a tape. Schools invested in science labs so that students could learn biology and physics in hands-on ways. In language labs, students heard recordings and practiced their pronunciation as they learned another language.

Teachers also developed new techniques. They began to emphasize group work so students could learn how to work with others. Many teachers stopped giving traditional multiple-choice tests and long term papers. Instead, they assigned projects that gave students a wide choice of products they could create. Often students used the new technologies to do these projects. For instance, students might make a video or design a computer presentation that combined words, pictures, and sounds. Educators called these different approaches "alternative assessment."

The ideas of psychologist Howard Gardner helped spur this movement. In 1983, Gardner published *Frames of Mind*. In it, he wrote that people have different kinds of intelligence. Some are more gifted working with words and others better with numbers.

A librarian helps a New Rochelle, New York student use the computer.
(© Tony Arruza/CORBIS)

Some, like dancers and athletes, have physical talents. Others are more skilled at relating to other people. Gardner argued that people learn more effectively when taught in ways that reach their particular kind of intelligence. Spurred by these ideas, teachers presented their lessons in different ways so they could reach students with different intelligences. The greater variety of projects was also meant to appeal to the variety of intelligences.

Problems in the Schools

Many schools became lively places where excited students used new technologies to learn—and show their learning—in new ways. Nevertheless, the nation's schools had many problems. Soon after taking office, President Ronald Reagan formed a commission to study education. In 1983, that group issued a gloomy report. Titled *A Nation at Risk*, the report said that the schools were doing a poor job preparing American children to work and become citizens. The report darkly said, "the educational foundations of our society are presently being eroded by a rising tide of mediocrity that threatens our very future as a Nation and a people."

The report—and other studies—highlighted several problems in America's schools. Of course, all schools did not have all these problems. Still, children, parents, educators, and political leaders worried about several issues.

First, many schools were overcrowded. In some suburbs, rapid population growth put more children into the school system than there was room. Some districts had to buy modular housing to hold classes. The problem was worse in the nation's cities. There, schools that had been built decades earlier were filled with more students than they could handle. Principals had to juggle to create spaces that could be used for classes. In some, several classes were crammed into a school auditorium or gym. In others, classes were even held in hallways.

Even worse, many city schools buildings were falling apart. Problems such as peeling paint, broken blackboards, heating systems that did not work, and even sewage water inside the buildings made these schools unpleasant—and even unhealthy. Schools lucky enough to avoid these problems often lacked material needed to carry out class. Science rooms did not have lab equipment. Students in many classes had to share textbooks, and those books were often out of date. Solving these problems would cost many

State Spending on Public Schools, 2000

The chart below shows the average amount spent on a public school student in the year 2000.

1. New Jersey	$9,588	19. Wyoming	$5,971	36. Kentucky	$5,155
2. Connecticut	$8,580	20. Ohio	$5,935	37. Nevada	$5,084
3. New York	$8,525	U.S. AVERAGE	$5,923	38. South Carolina	$5,050
4. Alaska	$8,231	21. New Hampshire	$5,920	38. North Carolina	$4,929
5. Dist. of Columbia	$8,048	21. Oregon	$5,920	40. Oklahoma	$4,817
6. Rhode Island	$7,612	23. Nebraska	$5,848	41. North Dakota	$4,808
7. Massachusetts	$7,331	24. Virginia	$5,788	42. Louisiana	$4,724
8. Delaware	$7,135	25. Iowa	$5,738	43. New Mexico	$4,682
9. Pennsylvania	$7,106	26. Washington	$5,734	44. Tennessee	$4,581
10. Michigan	$6,932	27. Hawaii	$5,633	45. Alabama	$4,595
11. Wisconsin	$6,796	28. Kansas	$5,508	46. Arkansas	$4,535
12. Vermont	$6,753	29. Montana	$5,481	47. Idaho	$4,447
13. Maryland	$6,755	30. Georgia	$5,369	48. Arizona	$4,413
14. Maine	$6,327	31. Florida	$5,360	49. South Dakota	$4,375
15. Indiana	$6,161	32. Colorado	$5,312	50. Mississippi	$4,039
16. West Virginia	$6,076	33. Missouri	$5,304	51. Utah	$3,783
17. Minnesota	$6,005	34. Texas	$5,267		
18. Illinois	$5,940	35. California	$5,260		

Source: National Center for Education Statistics

millions of dollars. But the cities did not have the money, and state legislatures were unwilling to raise taxes across the state to help the cities. In the late 1990s, President Bill Clinton proposed using federal money to rebuild schools. Congress did not pass his proposal, though.

The problems were particularly severe in city schools because cities had less money for education than suburbs did. In New York State, the wealthiest school district spent more than $38,000 for each student in the system. In the poorest school district, spending was under $5,500 per student. Texas had a similar gap, with wealthy districts spending $42,000 for each student and poorer districts at barely $3,000. The same was true in many states across the country. Those wealthy districts were generally suburbs. The poor districts were cities.

The results of this difference became clear in a comparison of two New Jersey elementary schools, one in a city and one in a suburb. The city school was 27 years older than the suburban school. It had nearly twice as many children jammed into less than half the space. Some New Jersey parents sued the state. They charged that the education of city children was not equal to that of suburban children. The state, they said, was not meeting its responsibility to educate all children. In 1988, a judge agreed. The ruling pointed out countless examples of poor-quality facilities, materials, and equipment in city schools. Courts in California, Ohio, Kentucky, Texas, and other states heard similar cases. In almost every state, the courts ruled that the state government had to take steps to make school funding more equal. Still, it took several years for the state legislatures to pass laws that the courts agreed would solve the problem.

City and suburban schools differed in another way—race. In 1954, the Supreme Court had ruled that laws creating separate schools for white and black students were unconstitutional. At the same time, whites continued to leave the cities for the suburbs. In the 1960s and 1970s, schools districts across the country took steps to integrate schools. This gave them a mix of white and black students. Some of these plans included busing students between cities and suburbs. In the 1980s and 1990s, the Court changed directions. Segregation remained illegal. But the Court put limits on what school districts could do to end it. The Court said that busing could not be used between city and suburban schools.

After these decisions, busing was largely stopped. As a result, the school systems became, in effect, segregated. Schools in suburbs, which were mostly white, had mostly white students. The cities increasingly became home to members of minority groups. As a result, growing numbers of black, Hispanic, and Asian students went to schools with very few white students. Meanwhile, nearly two-thirds of white students went to schools that were 90 percent or more white.

The Technology Gap

As technology came into greater use in the classroom, another problem arose. Poorer schools suffered from a technology gap. They did not have as many computers as suburban schools, and those they had were often not as up to date. Many of these schools did not have Internet access, closing students off from a wealth of information. President Clinton launched an effort in the 1990s to try to narrow this gap. The plan worked. By the end of the 1990s, more than 40 percent of schools with mostly minority students had Internet access. That was up from only 3 percent just four years earlier.

Changing the Schools

During the two decades, many efforts were made to solve the problems in the nation's schools. But each step roused heated debate. Educators and political leaders could not agree on what to do.

One approach was to push for tougher standards. Some critics said that the practice of social promotion was hurting students. Teachers, they said, passed students from one grade to the next even if they had not learned the year's lessons. They did so to keep students with others their same age. Critics of this practice pointed to studies showing that large numbers of high-school graduates could not read. Schools, they said, should create tests that students had to pass before they could advance to the next grade. This move became popular after 1989. That year, President George Bush met with the governors of all fifty states to talk about education. The idea of putting tests in place was widely discussed. Soon after, several states passed laws requiring students to be tested at several different grades.

These tests themselves drew criticism. Some observers said that relying on tests ignored some of the advances that had been made in education. The use of alternative assessments and project-based learning, they said, was dropping. Even worse, critics said, the tests hurt learning. Rather than teaching students what they needed to know, teachers only taught what students needed to know to pass the test.

Another approach to improving education focused on teachers. Some reformers wanted teachers' pay to be linked to their students' performance. Teachers whose classes scored well on tests would receive bigger raises. Those whose students performed poorly received no raises—or even faced losing their jobs. Many teachers did not like these plans. They argued that the problems of many students had little to do with the ability of their teachers. Often, students suffered from poverty, unsafe neighborhoods, and family troubles that hurt their ability to learn.

Other reformers tried to change schools. Some large cities brought in outside groups to run troubled schools. In some cases, local universities took charge. In other cases, private companies took control. This movement was called "privatization." The first experiment with this approach was in Baltimore, Maryland. The company managed to improve conditions in a school and bring in new computers and other advances. Students' perform-ance did not greatly improve, though. After only three years, the city cancelled the experiment. Other cities did try putting private companies in charge of one school or a few. By the end of the decade, it was not clear if this approach would produce the desired results.

Another approach was creating "charter schools." These were experimental schools in which a group of parents or teachers designed a new school. The group received a charter from the state to put their plan into effect. Charters covered three or five years. At the end of that period, the group had to apply to have the charter renewed. Some educators said the way to improve educa-tion was smaller classes. The average number of students in a class rose in the 1980s. With smaller classes, some educators said, teachers could focus more on each student—and give each one a better education. Studies supported this claim. Students in smaller classes did better on tests. Several states provided money for school districts that moved to lower class size. The results were uneven,

Students work on laptop computers at the Discovery Charter School in Tracy, California. The school is the first in the country to use a "paperless" system with all students using laptops with wireless connections to a server that carries all the daily lessons. (Photo by Justin Sullivan/Getty Images)

though. The programs had success in some states. In California, smaller classes had little positive effect. This was thought to be because well-trained teachers were not hired. The class size debate suffered from another problem. Reducing class size was one of the most costly ways of making schools better. That's because it meant building new schools and hiring more teachers.

Another debate raged over how to teach the growing number of students who did not speak English. Latin Americans and Asians made up most of the soaring number of immigrants coming to America in the 1980s and 1990s. As a result, schools had to teach large numbers of students who spoke hundreds of foreign languages and dialects. Many schools used bilingual education. "Bilingual" means speaking two languages. In these programs, reading and writing were taught in English. At the same time, students were taught in other subjects in their native language. Latino children, for example, learned math, science, and social studies in Spanish. The goal was to end the second-language instruction once students' English reading and writing skills became strong enough to study in English full time.

Some critics attacked these programs. They charged that the schools gave too little focus to teaching English. They said that students stayed in their foreign language classes for too many years. In California, critics launched a campaign to end bilingual programs. In 1998, California voters approved a law that called on school systems to more quickly move students whose main language was not English into English-only classrooms.

Private Schools

Meanwhile, growing numbers of children went to private schools. One attraction of many was that they had smaller class sizes. Many private schools had tough academic programs. They aimed at getting students ready for the top colleges in the country. The push for these elite schools had an impact in high school. Many parents believed that going to the more challenging private schools would give their children an edge for getting into those top colleges. As a result, applications to the private high schools went up.

Many private schools were run by a church. They added some kind of religious teaching to regular classes. Religious schools became the focus of a debate over another school reform idea. Some critics of public schools urged states to offer parents vouchers. In a voucher plan, the government gives parents a small sum of money that they can use to pay the tuition charged by a private school. Vouchers were supposed to make private school more of an option for poor people. Supporters said that this gave poor people more freedom of choice. By giving these parents an option, supporters said, public schools would be forced to get better. Otherwise those schools would lose students.

Critics of this idea had several arguments against vouchers. They said that the amount in most plans was not enough to pay for top-quality schools. They said that losing students would only hurt public schools more, not improve them. Finally, they argued that vouchers used to pay for religious schools violated the Constitution, the basic law of the land. The Constitution bans the government from supporting any particular church or religion. If vouchers are used to pay for religious schools, critics said, the government would, in effect, be supporting a religion. Despite these objections, vouchers were put in place in some states. As with other school reforms, it would take some years before the results could be tested.

Preschool

One area of great change was preschool—education before first grade. By the late 1990s, More than half of all children three and four years old were going to a nursery school. Nearly nine million children went to a nursery school or a kindergarten class. These numbers showed a dramatic change over the past. In 1965, only 11 percent of all three and four year olds were in nursery school. Only about two million children attended nursery schools and kindergarten.

There were two main reasons for these major changes. First, by the late 1990s, nearly two-thirds of all women with children under six worked outside the home. These working mothers needed child care. Putting children in school became the choice for many.

The other reason was the existence of Head Start, a preschool program. This program was started in the 1960s by the federal government. The goal was to improve the health and education of poor children. Parents also took part as aides to teachers. The hope was that by becoming prepared for school, they would gain skills that led to better jobs. By the late 1990s, more than 800,000 children took part in Head Start. The program was not perfect. It could not provide places for all children who could attend—there was not enough money. The pay for Head Start teachers was low, making it difficult to recruit or keep the best teachers. Some classes were better than others. Despite these problems, tests showed that Head Start helped poor children. The program enjoyed widespread support.

Social Problems

America's schools were part of American society. Some of the problems in that society found their way into the schools. One of those problems was violence. Throughout the two decades, there were alarming stories about students bringing dangerous weapons into schools. Some carried knives; others brought guns. In some schools, officials installed metal detectors at the entrance doors. These devices sounded an alarm whenever a person carrying a weapon passed through them. Some schools went so far as to require students to carry clear book bags. That way, school officials could easily see that students were not hiding any weapons.

Worried officials also took other steps. Many schools began to teach students about ways to keep disagreements from turning violent. Some put in place programs aimed at helping students settle disagreements. If two students were caught up in a conflict, they could meet with a mediator. That was another student, trained to handle such situations. That mediator oversaw the meeting and helped them reach a settlement.

Still, some students made no effort to settle their conflicts. A few bitterly angry students caused deadly damage. Starting in 1996, there was a rash of school shootings. In some cases, the shooters killed or wounded several people, both students and teachers. The shootings occurred in many different communities, from Mississippi to Oregon.

The worst one took place in 1999 at Columbine High School in Littleton, Colorado. On April 20, two boys carried out a plan they had secretly been hatching for months. Armed with shotguns, the two went on a killing spree that terrorized students and teachers. They killed twelve students and a teacher and wounded thirty more. Finally, they killed themselves.

A memorial service at Columbine High School in Littleton, Colorado.
(© AFP/CORBIS)

Shocked Americans were left with many questions. Why did they do it? How had they planned for so long without anyone knowing of their plot? What had their parents done?

The two were fans of violent computer games. Some critics charged that those games numbed the two killers to accept violence. Others argued against that explanation. Millions of teens play the games for long hours, they pointed out. But the vast majority knew better than to pick up real guns and shoot real people. Others said that the shootings proved it was too easy for people to get guns. The Columbine shooting renewed calls for laws limiting gun sales. (See Chapter 2 for more on this issue). Again, though, there were many teens across the country who had access to guns but did not turn them on their classmates.

Clearly, the two teens had serious emotional problems. Another student at Columbine High said that the two killers were "anti-everything." They apparently felt rejected by other students. In fact, they picked out students who belonged to the school's more popular groups—athletes, for instance—as their targets. Some people said that the school itself was part of the problem. Columbine was a very large and impersonal school. It was easy there for two troubled boys to escape the notice of people who could help them learn to handle their problems.

While people struggled to explain Columbine, worried parents and school officials had another concern. They wanted to make sure that another shooting would not take place in their own schools. Many school systems put in place "zero tolerance" rules. They said that no student could bring into school anything that might be a weapon, without exception. They cracked down on students who even suggested a threat to other students. Some responses might have been extreme. In one case, school officials seized a student's nail clipper. They said that the tool could be used to stab a classmate. Such actions underscored how very scared school officials and parents were.

Higher Education

While primary and secondary schools remained largely segregated, predominantly white colleges tried to attract more students of color. The programs they put in place were called "affirmative action." As discussed in Chapter 2, education became a key battleground on this issue.

Taking into account past discrimination, colleges often accepted lower grades from minority students. Opponents of affirmative action said this created reverse discrimination. That is, bringing more minorities into college hurt the chances of white students with equal or better qualifications. In several cases, the Supreme Court put limits on how race could be used in making decisions about college acceptance. In the late 1990s, California voters went further. They approved a law that banned using preferences for women or minorities when making college admissions decisions. Many critics said that this action would force colleges to exclude many minority students.

Despite these challenges, college students were more diverse than ever before. In 1999, minority students were about one-third of all college students. This was nearly double the rate in 1976. As a result, a greater share of people in minorities had college educations. African Americans showed great gains. In 1960, only about 3 percent of all blacks had a college degree. By 1999, that rate had jumped five times to more than 15 percent. The increase for Hispanics, or Latinos, was less dramatic. Among people of a Spanish-speaking background, the percentage of college graduates doubled from just under 5 percent in 1970 to just over 10 percent in 1999.

With a few exceptions, increases in female college attendance caused less controversy than issues of race. From 1960 to the late 1990s, the percentage of men who had a college degree nearly tripled, from just under 10 percent to over 26 percent. The percentage of women with a college degree, though, jumped almost four times, from under 6 percent to more than 22 percent. And women seemed determined to close the remaining gap. By the end of the period, women made up more than half of all people getting college degrees.

Another change was the age of college students. Most college students were between 18 and 23 years old. Still, by the late 1990s, more than 40 percent were older. Most of these adults were taking courses to further their careers.

The cost of a college education went up dramatically in this period. Between 1985 and 1999, the cost of attending a four-year public college—such as a state university—more than doubled. For private colleges, costs shot up more than two and a half times to top $25,000. The elite private schools—places like Harvard and Yale—cost more than $30,000 a year. The cost of books, other materials, and various fees added to this expense. Students who wanted even more schooling—at medical or law school, for instance—faced added costs.

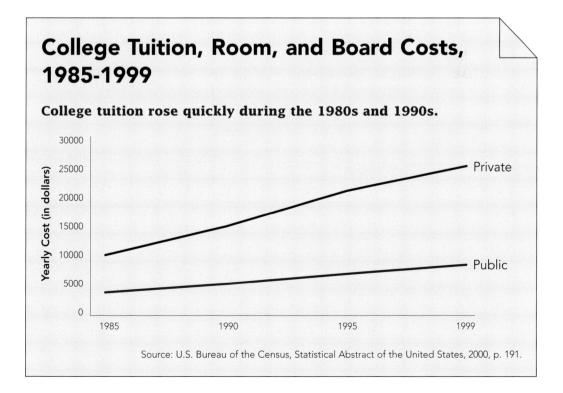

College Tuition, Room, and Board Costs, 1985-1999

College tuition rose quickly during the 1980s and 1990s.

Source: U.S. Bureau of the Census, Statistical Abstract of the United States, 2000, p. 191.

The government wanted to encourage people to go to college. One way was to make it easier for students—and parents—to meet these rising costs. Many states passed laws that allowed people to set up education savings accounts. The states promised not to tax any money that parents put in these accounts. Parents could save the money for years, until children finally reached college age. A growing share of students borrowed the money they needed. Of course, those loans eventually had to be repaid, but not until after graduation. And people with college degrees earned more than those who had only finished high school.

Still, the cost of college was too high for many Americans. Some chose to go to two-year schools, such as community colleges. Some simply used these two-year degrees to launch their work life. Others went to these less costly schools for two years and then transferred to a four-year school to complete their degree work.

The Internet gave rise to another new movement in higher education—distance learning. Students could use their computers to log onto an Internet site devoted to a particular course. There, they could tap into a variety of resources. They could view lectures, obtain assignments, and even take tests and participate in class discussions. Some schools let students take all the courses needed to earn a degree in this way.

Distance learning was popular with working adults. Online, they could learn new job skills—or prepare for a new career. Since the material was provided online, they could do the work at any time.

As the United States entered the twenty-first century, education still had many growing pains. Yet no one could ignore its importance.

Chapter Four

The Economy

The American economy began to change dramatically in the late 1900s. One of those changes was in its make-up. In the 1800s, the economy had changed from agriculture to industry. Now it was changing again—from heavy industry to one of service industries. This category includes government, retail sales, transportation, communications, finance, and personal services. In the late 1900s, the number of factory workers dropped from a high of just over 20 million to under 19 million. At the same time, the number of service workers soared. By the late 1990s, service jobs had increased by nearly three times. They outnumbered factory jobs by more than five to one.

What happened to those factory jobs? In large part, they were shipped outside the country. Companies closed factories in the United States and opened them in other countries. The reason was simple: they could pay foreign workers a small fraction of what American workers earned. Workers in South Korea, Hong Kong, and Taiwan earned just a third of what American workers did. Mexican workers were paid just a tenth.

General Motors cut its workforce from 500,000 people in the 1970s to just over 300,000 in the mid-1990s. Boeing—a highly successful maker of airplanes—cut nearly 50,000 jobs in the 1990s. In some cases, whole industries were nearly wiped out. American factories making such products as shoes, televisions, textiles, and

During the 1980s and 1990s, the stock market had several dramatic rises and falls. In the photograph above (LEFT) stock traders at the American Stock Exchange watch the performance of their stocks (© CORBIS). During the 1990s, more and more Americans used the Internet (RIGHT) for online shopping. (Brand X Pictures) telephones almost disappeared. Instead, foreign workers made all these products, which were then imported into the United States. As journalists Donald Bartlett and James Steele wrote,

> In your closet, the Bugle Boy blue jeans came from Nicaragua. The Speedo swimming trunks were made in China and Malaysia. The Reeboks in Thailand and Indonesia. The Ralph Lauren Chaps sweatshirt in Pakistan. The Starter official U.S. Olympic baseball cap—inscribed "Bringing America Together"—was made in the Dominican Republic. The great American leisure-time uniform: sweatshirt, blue jeans, baseball cap, sneakers. All made offshore.

Another change was the continued drop in the importance of agriculture. Early in the 1900s, farm products made up nearly a quarter of the nation's economic output. By the end of the century, agriculture's share of national production was a mere 1 percent. The farm world was changing in other ways, too. The family farm almost vanished. There were fewer farms, but they tended to be larger—the average size of a farm jumped from 297 acres in 1960 to more than 430 acres by 1998. Large companies—what was called "agri-business"—had taken over farming. But farm production had gone way up. Farmers grew more than even a growing population could eat. They had to rely on selling food overseas. In 1960, farmers only sold $3.1 billion worth of food abroad. By 1998, they were shipping $53.7 billion to other countries.

The economy had stumbled in the 1970s, as the country was mired in a recession.

Rising oil prices had made business's costs jump. High interest rates had made it expensive for companies to borrow money. High interest rates and high prices also held down consumer spending. Businesses—with less demand for their goods and services—cut back on production. They laid off many workers. The country was in a period of slow economic activity called a recession. Ronald Reagan, running for president in 1980, noted the high rates of unemployment rate and inflation, or rising prices. He called the result the "misery index" and blamed President Jimmy Carter for the fact that this index was going up. Reagan promised better times ahead with a joke: "A recession is when your neighbor loses his job and a depression is when you lose your job. Recovery is when Jimmy Carter loses his!" When he took office, Reagan launched a massive increase in defense spending. This hike in government spending did boost the economy, which grew every year from 1982 to 1990.

But Reagan combined high spending with deep tax cuts. As a result, the federal government spent more money than it took in every year. This forced the government to borrow money to pay for the added spending. The result was a huge deficit (the difference between income and spending.) By 1992, the government had to borrow nearly $300 billion. Some economists said this borrowing cut down on the amount of money businesses could borrow. As a result, they could not expand, which meant that they could not create more jobs. In addition, the government had to pay interest on its debt. By 1990, those payments totaled as much as $60 billion a year—money the government could not use to provide services. Many political leaders began to worry about these deficits. Finally, in 1987, Congress passed a law that required the government to balance the budget—making spending equal to receipts—by 1993.

In the early 1990s, another recession hit. This one lasted a little less than a year, but it came just as President George Bush was running for re-election. Voters felt that Bush did little to try to fix the slumping economy. Energetic Democrat Bill Clinton won the election in the fall of 1992. Clinton had good luck—he took office as the economy was already growing again. He also made good policy decisions, which helped that growth. He decided not to cut taxes and increased federal spending to create construction jobs across the country.

This stand helped gain the confidence of Alan Greenspan, the chairman of the Federal Reserve Board. The "Fed" is the nation's central bank. It sets rules that control interest rates and the money supply. Under Greenspan, the Fed cut interest rates. Business owners began to borrow and invest money to help their companies grow. One major investment was new technology. The personal computer had appeared in 1981. Soon, businesspeople began to use the new machines, finding new ways of doing work faster and more efficiently. Workers became more productive, able to finish more work in the same amount of time as before. This rise in productivity lowered the cost of doing business. Business profits rose. The economy began to grow at a faster rate. From 1992 until the end of the decade, the economy grew each year. Clinton took credit, calling it the longest period of sustained

Alan Greenspan
(Library of Congress)

growth in the country's history.

The economic boom brought more jobs to more people. During most of the 1980s, the unemployment rate—the percentage of people who wanted a job but could not find one—was 6 percent or higher. After a dip late in the decade, the rate spiked again in the early 1990s. It reached a high of 7.5 percent in the recession year of 1992. Once the economy recovered, though, the jobless rate started to drop. By 1999, only 4.2 percent of workers did not have a job. It was the lowest rate in thirty years.

The United States seemed to have weathered the economic problems of the 1970s and 1980s. It still had the largest economy in the world—by far. As the table on page 68 shows, the American GDP was larger than those of the second and third largest economies combined. GDP is gross domestic product, the total value of all goods and services produced and sold within a country.

Most remarkably, the economy generated a huge number of jobs. In 1980, just under 100 million people had jobs. By the late 1990s, that number had grown to more than 130 million. Despite all the gloomy news for many years, then, the 1990s seemed to show a highly successful economy.

Still, there were some troubling signs. One problem was the growing gulf between rich and poor Americans. In the 1980s and 1990s, the wealthiest families saw their income go up at a much higher rate than poorer families. In 1992, 90 percent of all Americans controlled only 61 percent of the nation's total income. That was down seven points from 1980.

Another troubling sign was the steep drop in the amount of money Americans saved. In 1975, Americans saved 9 percent of their income. That rate fell steadily until, by 1999, they were saving only 2.2 percent—just over two cents of every dollar. Some people simply did not earn enough to save. Others had to dip into their savings in order to get by. At the same time, consumers were borrowing more than ever before. Some consumers used credit cards to buy luxury items or to travel. Some needed them just to meet regular expenses or medical emergencies. For some, the mountain of debt proved disastrous when they lost their jobs and could not meet credit payments. Throughout the 1990s, a growing number of people had to declare bankruptcy—meaning they could not pay off their debts.

Another problem was the country's soaring trade deficit. The value of the goods the country imported was larger than the value of its exports. Throughout the 1980s and 1990s, Americans bought more foreign goods than the nation sold to other countries. Some economists said that these trade deficits weakened the American economy. Because of the deficits, foreigners held a large supply of American dollars. Others said there was nothing wrong with that. The foreigners would simply invest those dollars in the United States by buying land or companies. Then it would be in their interest to help the American economy grow so that the investments would pay off.

It's a Small World, After All

While this debate raged, one fact became clear. The economies of the world were increasingly tied together. The United States had long supported the goal of free trade—the removal of barriers to trade between countries. The aim was to create new markets abroad for American products. In many ways, the strategy worked. American exports increased eleven times from 1960 to 1980, from $20 billion to $220 billion. By the end of the century, they had soared to nearly $700 billion. American blue jeans, cigarettes, and cola drinks became popular around the world. McDonald's enjoyed amazing success, spreading to 120 countries and serving around 40 million customers a day. American television shows, movies, singers, and athletes gained worldwide success. Basketball star Michael Jordan became world famous, and people in Africa and China eagerly bought jerseys with his number.

Of course, globalization—the growing interdependence of the world's economies—cut both ways. Free trade also gave Americans more access to goods made abroad—and they were happy to buy them. Nowhere was the change more evident than in the auto industry. In the 1950s and 1960s, American car makers enjoyed boom times. In 1960, the Big Three American auto companies—General Motors, Ford, and Chrysler—sold 92 out of every 100 cars bought in the United States. But these companies suffered two major blows in the 1970s. The oil crisis raised the demand for cars that used less gasoline. Since few American cars qualified, consumers began to buy cars made in Japan and Germany. The second jolt was a decline in the quality of American-made cars.

The World's Largest Economies, 1998

COUNTRY	GDP (billions of dollars)
1. United States	$8,511
2. China	4,420
3. Japan	2,903
4. Germany	1,813
5. India	1,689
6. France	1,320
7. United Kingdom	1,252
8. Italy	1,181
9. Brazil	1,035
10. Mexico	815

Source: CIA World Factbook

American automakers watched their share of the car market shrink each year.

They changed to become more competitive—and it worked. In the 1980s, they built more cars that burned less gasoline than before. (In the 1990s, the car makers sold more trucks and heavier cars that guzzled gas. But the fuel crisis was over by then, and the public bought the cars gladly.) U.S. manufacturers improved the quality of their cars. Still, the big automakers faced a new world. By the late 1990s, cars made abroad accounted for 53 of every 100 cars bought each year in the United States. However, half of those 53 cars were manufactured in Canada or Mexico in plants owned by American car companies. So the figure was not quite as bad as it looked.

On the other hand, Japanese and German car companies had their own factories in the United States. And those factories built cars that cut into American car sales. And one of the Big Three was no longer an American company. In 1998, the German car company Daimler-Benz merged with Chrysler. While the new company was supposed to be an equal partnership between the two firms, German executives dominated it.

Auto sales were just part of a growing problem between the United States and Japan. During the 1970s and 1980s, the United States developed a huge trade deficit with Japan. There were two reasons. First, American consumers bought growing numbers of Japanese cars—and televisions, videocassette recorders, stereos, cameras, computers, and other electronic equipment. Second, Japan blocked American companies from selling their goods in Japan. The American government tried to convince Japan to loosen those trade barriers. But the trade deficit continued to soar. Japan was not the only Asian economy that created problems for the United States. In the late 1980s and 1990s, the Chinese economy passed Japan to become the world's second largest. Throughout these years, the United States imported more and more goods from China. Its trade deficit with that country soared. By the middle 1990s, it had reached more than $30 billion a year.

The American effort to convince Japan to drop trade barriers was part of a larger movement taking place around the world. Countries were signing trade agreements that linked their economies. The largest of these trade blocs was the European Community, which included 15 members in Western Europe. These countries agreed to break down trade barriers for each other's goods. In the process, they created one of the world's largest markets. Most of the countries even agreed to use a common currency. They dropped their old national money systems in favor of a new euro.

American leaders grew concerned that a unified European market could become a major economic competitor. So they began to push for a regional trade bloc in North America. The result was the North American Free Trade Agreement (NAFTA), signed by the United States, Mexico, and Canada. The plan called for the three countries to cut down all trade barriers for each other. In 1991, President George Bush predicted that NAFTA would bring great benefits to American workers:

> I don't have to tell anyone about Mexico's market potential: 85 million consumers who want to buy our goods. Nor do I have to tell you that as Mexico grows and prospers, it will need even more of the goods we're best at producing: computers, manufacturing equipment, high-tech and high-value products.

Not everyone agreed. Labor unions said that open trade with Mexico would lead to the loss of even more American jobs. But when Bill Clinton was elected president in 1992, he supported NAFTA, too. In 1993, Congress voted to approve the trade treaty. The effects were immediate. American exports to Mexico did rise—but imports from Mexico rose even faster. Until 1994, the United States had enjoyed a trade surplus with Mexico. Starting in 1995, America imported far more goods from Mexico than it sold there. By 1999, the American trade deficit with Mexico reached nearly $23 billion.

While American workers might have suffered from these changes, American companies were thriving. Huge corporations like General Electric, General Motors, Ford, Exxon, IBM, Wal-

In 1994, the U.S. Congress approved the North American Free Trade Agreement (NAFTA). The agreement helped encourage American businesses to open factories south of the border in Mexico where wages are lower. Many Americans, especially members of labor unions, opposed NAFTA for this reason. (Library of Congress)

Mart, and Mobil still ranked among the largest corporations in the world. Indeed, nearly a third of the world's top 500 corporations were American. With operations in many countries, it did not matter if their American workforce got smaller. General Motors shipped fewer than 100,000 American-made cars to other countries in a year. Yet it had nearly $50 billion in sales outside the United States. It simply made the cars in other countries.

The growing globalization had its critics. Some people charged that the giant multinational corporations no longer had any loyalty to their home countries. They were only interested in making money and would do anything to achieve that goal, even if it meant going against the interests of their original national home. Critics said that the multinationals took unfair advantage of people in poor countries by paying them low wages and forcing them to work in unpleasant factories. They said that the multinationals moved to poorer countries so they could avoid laws limiting pollution. And, they said, the multinationals were destroying the unique cultures of the world by making every place look the same.

The criticism reached a peak in 1999. That year, the World Trade Organization (WTO) met in Seattle, Washington. The WTO—which counted most countries as members—aimed to promote world trade. But critics said that WTO actions simply made it easier for multinationals to take over the world's economy. When the trade ministers of scores of countries gathered in Seattle for the 1999 WTO meeting, they were met by protesters. An estimated 50,000 activists took to the streets. They chanted slogans and staged demonstrations against globalization and multinational companies.

Supporters of globalization countered the criticisms. They said that global companies helped spread ideas of human dignity and democratic values. They granted that the wages paid to factory workers in Malaysia or Mexico were lower than those paid in the United States or Western Europe. But they pointed out that those workers were still better off than others in their countries. As economist Paul Krugman said, "To claim that [these workers] have been impoverished by globalization . . . you have to forget that those workers were even poorer before . . . and ignore the fact that those who do not have access to global markets are far worse off than those who do." Whatever the arguments, globalization was happening, and very quickly.

Wall Street Wonders

While economic news was being made all over the world, much of it came out of Wall Street, the New York home of American financial markets. Stocks and bonds were bought and sold there. When investors buy stock, they buy part ownership in a corporation. When they buy bonds, they are, in effect, lending the corporation money. All that buying and selling made several headlines in the 1980s and 1990s.

In the early 1980s, the bond markets were busier than the stock market. In those years, interest rates were high. That meant that people could make more money from bonds than they could from stocks. About 1984, though, stocks began to look better as an investment, and the stock market began to rise. The Dow Jones Industrial Average tracks the value of a select group of important stocks, which shows overall trends in the market. The Dow jumped more than 300 points from 1984 to 1985 and another 300 by 1986—and it kept climbing. Investors were jubilant—until "Black Monday." On Monday, October 19, 1987, so many people sold stock that the Dow fell 508 points. It was the biggest one-day drop in history, as stocks lost nearly a fifth of their value. Fortunately, the market rallied over the next few days.

The 1987 stock market crash was a jolt to investors' confidence, but only a brief one. The market began to rise again, and did so steadily—and sharply—throughout the 1990s. New record highs were set at a dizzying pace, and the Dow Jones average eventually passed the 11,000 mark, a fivefold increase over the level in 1988. Three factors fueled this surge. First, the economy was growing faster than it had in the 1980s. Second, the federal government was showing budget surpluses—taking in more money than it spent. That increased confidence in the economy and drove interest rates down, making stocks more attractive than bonds. Third, the rise in Internet use was attracting new, and exciting, business opportunities. Many companies—called "dot-coms" for their World Wide Web domain name—formed in the 1990s to make money off the Internet. To get the funds to grow, they offered stock to the public. The initial stock sales generated millions for the company's owners. Later stock trading drove prices up even higher, making millions—on paper—for many people.

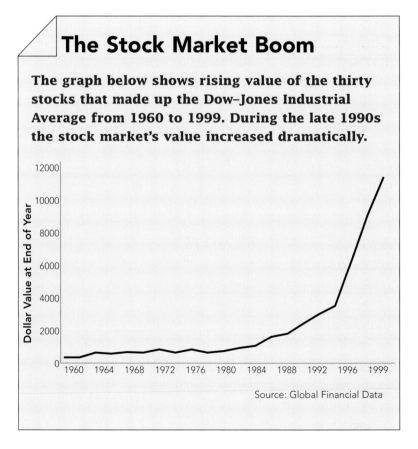

The Stock Market Boom

The graph below shows rising value of the thirty stocks that made up the Dow–Jones Industrial Average from 1960 to 1999. During the late 1990s the stock market's value increased dramatically.

Source: Global Financial Data

Not everyone was thrilled with the 1990s stock boom. Alan Greenspan warned that the soaring stock prices might reveal too much optimism. In 1996, he spoke of "irrational exuberance"—that is, investors letting their emotions get the better of their judgment. As stock prices continued to soar, many experts thought Greenspan was being too gloomy. After the turn of the century, the stock market fell far and fast. Then the old economist looked pretty smart.

During the 1990s, though, the stock market still looked attractive. It began to attract more people than ever before. In the past, most Americans looked on Wall Street trading as an interesting diversion but something remote from their lives. That changed in the late 1900s. By the late 1990s, 52 percent of all Americans—more than one out of every two—owned stock. As late as 1980, the rate had only been 13 percent, or one out of every eight people. The main spur to this growth was the spread of retirement funds. These are funds that people invest in during their working years. Then, when they retire, the money is available to meet living expenses. Many companies set up retirement funds for their workers. In most cases, employers matched some money contributed by workers. As the stock market kept rising, the funds owned by many people rose in value.

New Winners and Losers

Business is a competitive world, with winners and losers. Some of those winners in the 1980s and 1990s were familiar names. These companies had dominated business for much of the century. General Electric thrived under the dynamic leadership of Jack Welch. Ford rebounded from troubled times to challenge General Motors as the leading car company. Oil companies remained successful. Boeing, the aircraft manufacturer, was another highly successful company—although it was increasingly challenged by foreign airplane makers.

Some of the winners in the late 1990s were newcomers. One of these was retailer Wal-Mart. Founder Sam Walton's idea was to create huge stores that sold a great variety of products at very low prices. He did it by setting up giant warehouses that could feed several stores. Because his warehouses were so large, he could buy goods in large quantities at low prices. He passed those savings on to consumers. He also located his stores in rural areas, where there was little competition. The strategy worked, and Wal-Mart became the nation's largest retailer. In fact, it became one of the country's largest companies—only General Motors had higher sales. Wal-Mart was also one of the country's largest employers, with nearly one million workers. Falling far behind were traditional retail giants like Sears, J.C. Penneys, and department stores.

Other successful retailers followed the same strategy of selling goods at a high discount. Target and Kmart, like Wal-Mart, sold everything. Most of the discounters, though, specialized in a small range of goods. Toys R Us became the leading toy retailer. Home Depot and Lowe's led the "do-it-yourself" market. They set up large stores where people could buy hardware, paint, flooring, doors, windows, and anything else they wanted to fix up their homes. Best Buy and Circuit City sold consumer electronics, music, and movies. Barnes & Noble opened giant bookstores and welcomed browsers by decorating them with comfortable easy chairs and coffee service.

New companies also arose in the phone industry. AT&T had dominated the telephone business for years, doing everything from making phones to handling local and long distance calls. Then the government sued the company, charging that it was a trust that unfairly limited competition. In the early 1980s, a judge agreed and ordered the phone giant to be split into several different companies. Local service would be handled by seven regional phone companies, which were nicknamed "Baby Bells." AT&T would be allowed to sell long distance, but it also had to accept competition. Soon, new phone companies sprang up, with Sprint and MCI emerging as the strongest competitors against AT&T for long distance business.

The AT&T case broke up one of America's largest corporations, but the main trend in the 1980s and 1990s was for enlarging. Some of the growth came in the personal computer industry, which was born and flourished in this period. The biggest winner here was Microsoft, which produced software for the great majority of personal computers. Microsoft founder Bill Gates had signed an agreement with IBM to provide the operating system, the basic software, for the new personal computer it released in 1981. High sales of IBM computers—and the machines made by other companies that worked the same way—brought growing streams of revenue to Microsoft. The company branched out, creating programs for word processing and other business functions. In 1995, it launched a whole new operating system—Windows 95—in a worldwide party. By then, 90 percent of the world's computers were running on Microsoft software. The company sold nearly $20 billion worth of products a year by the end of the decade. Gates became one of the richest men in the world.

Microsoft was late getting into the Internet business, but once it did, it jumped in with a vengeance. The government then sued the company, charging that Microsoft had broken antitrust laws in trying to enter this market. A judge agreed with the government, and threatened to break the company up. But Microsoft appealed the decision to a higher court, and the judges there overturned that part of the judge's decision. Microsoft remained a giant.

The companies that made computers grew large as well. IBM actually dropped out of the personal computer business. Like Microsoft, newcomers Dell, Sun Systems, and Gateway were led by daring and smart founders. They started out small but grew to be major players. Internet companies like America Online and Yahoo! helped make the World Wide Web popular by giving people ways of connecting and moving through the mass of information. Amazon revolutionized retailing by creating an easy-to-use system for buying books online. It helped give birth to "e-commerce," or the buying of goods online. By the end of the decade, Internet sales totaled about $300 billion—nearly the same level as auto sales.

Bill Gates, founder and chairman of Microsoft Corporation
(Courtesy of Microsoft, Inc.)

The trend to bigness was seen in several mergers, or agreements to join companies together. Each year, it seemed, a new record was set for these deals. In 1994, AT&T bought a cell-phone company for $16.7 billion. Two years later, Walt Disney bought Capital Cities/ABC for $18.3 billion. In 1997, Bell Atlantic—one of the "Baby Bells"—acquired Nynex—another "Baby Bell"—for $30.8 billion. The next year, Travelers, an insurance business, bought Citicorp, a banking company, for a whopping $72.6 billion. The record was hit in 1999, when oil giant Exxon bought oil giant Mobil for $86.4 billion.

Some of the mergers aimed to achieve what executives called "synergies." This was especially the case in the joining of media companies, such as Disney and Capital Cities/ABC. Disney brought movies, music, and theme parks to the deal. Capital Cities/ABC had record companies, a television network, and various cable networks. These provided ways for Disney to get its movies and music to the public. Business leaders hoped to make deals between the different divisions of the new company that would hold down costs and let everyone share in the profits. At the same time, media companies were finding new ways to make money. Popular movies or television shows were exploited in new ways. The companies that owned them signed deals with toy companies, video-game makers, clothing firms, and fast-food restaurants. An avalanche of products hit the market.

The goal of many of these new mega-corporations was to reach into new businesses and to make operations more efficient. One way of achieving efficiency was to cut duplication—the number of similar products or services offered. There was plenty of that. The newly formed giants often had people in more than one place doing the same kind of work—work that earlier had been done for two different companies. So the big mergers were often followed by layoffs, as once-valuable workers were no longer needed. Corporate executives said they were "trimming fat from the payroll" and "cutting redundant operations." Wall Street investors applauded them for making "tough decisions" because profits rose. Meanwhile, tens of thousands of people suddenly found themselves without jobs. That was just one of the ways that the workplace changed in the 1980s and 1990s.

Chapter Five

Work

American businesses underwent many changes in the late 1900s. As a result, work changed in many ways, too. The two chief changes had to do with technology and the increasing competition brought on by globalization. New technologies made it possible to work faster—and at all hours. And the intense competition brought about changes in how companies were organized and in how work was done.

Office workers (LEFT) **gather to discuss business** (Photodisc). **Although most fire-fighters are men, some women have also joined fire-fighting companies, like this one** (RIGHT) **in New York City.** (Library of Congress)

Technology in the Workplace

The biggest change in workplace technology was the spread of the personal computer (PC). In 1980, workers still relied on typewriters and telephones. Reports had to be dictated or written out by hand and then laboriously typed, proofread, and corrected. The largest companies had computers, but these were generally large machines that were controlled by a highly skilled group of workers. Most employees did not have direct access to the data on these systems. Getting information could take days.

Computers changed all that. By the late 1990s, most office workers in most companies had computers on their desks. Workers used word-processing programs to write, edit, format, and print reports and other documents. The final product could include photographs and other illustrations, in full color. They looked far more professional than anything that came out of the typewriter era. Workers used electronic spreadsheets to make complex financial calculations. They could tap into the company's database of facts about products, services, and employees. With e-mail, they could quickly send messages to coworkers and clients. With Internet connections, they could tap into a wealth of information.

Business writers predicted that the new machines would bring about the "paperless office." That is, all work would be done and stored on a computer. There would no longer be a need for cumbersome paper files. While the paperless office never appeared, the spread of computers did revolutionize work. Employees who had more access to more information could make faster—and better—decisions. They could be more helpful when customers called in to ask about products or to check on the status of an order. Lightweight laptop computers kept sales workers who were always on the road in close contact with the home office.

But PCs changed more than just office work. Stores replaced cash registers with computer-driven machines. Now cashiers aimed lasers at the special bar codes imprinted on packages or tags. The code identified the product and instantly entered its price onto the computer.

This system was first used in supermarkets, but it quickly spread to many different kinds of stores. The new system gave stores several benefits. First, customer checkouts went more quickly and more accurately. Cashiers no longer had to input strings of numbers—which took away the chance of a cashier making an error. Second, stores could change prices and not have to worry about the cashier entering an old price. Whatever price was stored at that moment in the store's central computer was the price charged to the customer. Third, stores were able to keep an up-to-the-minute record of their inventory, or the supply of items they had for sale. Each time a customer bought a new pair of jeans, say, the store's database subtracted a pair—of the right brand and size—from the computer's record. In this way, purchasing workers could see when stocks in some items were falling low and order more.

Even manufacturing took to computers. Engineers began to use sophisticated programs to design new products. Some factories installed computer-driven robots on their assembly lines. The new machines became the new factory workers. They built the products. These complex robots cost a lot of money but provided many benefits. Robotic painters could be programmed to apply a certain amount of paint, holding down costs by never putting on too much. They never tired, which meant that quality could be upheld. And they could do work—like welding or painting—that was dangerous to workers' health.

Other workers found new ways to use computers. Busy people used tiny machines to store their schedules and the names and phone numbers of their key clients. Auto mechanics used computers so they could see if a car was working properly. Even farmers used computers. Some simply used them to handle their financial records. In the late 1900s, though, more and more came to use computers to decide such things as what crops to plant on what part of their fields and how much to fertilize.

Technology moved so quickly that some early machines of the period were virtually ignored later. In the 1980s, two changes made communications more rapid than ever. Federal Express created a new business based on the idea of guaranteed overnight

During the 1980s and 1990s, many factories, like this Honda automotive factory in Marysville, Ohio, began using robotic equipment to speed manufacturing. (Courtesy of Honda Motors)

delivery. Suddenly, workers in a New York company could send a report to people in a California company and know that the package would arrive by the next business morning. FedEx, as it came to be called, was born in the 1970s, but became highly successful in the 1980s. The next innovation made overnight delivery look slow. Facsimile (fax) machines used telephone lines to transmit images of the information on paper over long distances almost instantly. Now those New York workers could fax their report to California the same day. By the end of the 1990s, though, the Internet and e-mail had made even fax machines less necessary. Instead of printing out the report from their computer and then faxing it, a worker simply had to press a button to transmit the report by e-mail.

New Technologies Create New Problems

The spread of computerized technology raised new issues, though. Companies had to train their workers to use the new systems. New businesses sprang up to offer custom-made training sessions to large numbers of workers. The situation was complicated by the fight among the software companies to get more and more customers to buy their programs. Every few years, software publishers issued new versions of their programs. Each was an attempt to beat the competition by supplying more features that workers could use to do a greater variety of work. The result, though, was to create programs that grew harder to learn. They had to be relearned each time the company bought a new version.

Another problem was a health issue. Workers spent more and more time at a computer keyboard inputting information. As a result, some developed health problems. The most prominent was a problem in the hands called repetitive stress injury. The problem resulted from repeating the same motions over and over again for long periods of time day after day. This repetition caused swelling in tendons in the wrist and hands. The swollen tendons then put pressure on a nerve, which brought pain. That pain could be severe. Doctors found some ways to treat the condition. In some cases, though, workers needed surgery. And some workers had to find new jobs to get away from the repeated work that caused the problem.

Privacy also became an issue. In the 1990s, workers came to rely increasingly on e-mail for communication. Just as workers had often used the office phone to talk to family or friends, some used office e-mail systems to send personal messages. At the same time, some workers used their employer's high-speed Internet connections to handle personal matters, such as shopping for holiday presents or simply browsing the World Wide Web. New issues arose over whether workers had the right to maintain the privacy of their e-mail messages.

The new technologies took another toll. Faxes, computers, cell phones, and pagers meant that workers could always be contacted. The phrase "24/7" came into use. It referred to the new ability to be electronically in touch with the outside world twenty-four hours a day, seven days a week. But being always connected meant, for some workers, never getting away from work. Americans began working an increasing numbers of hours. A study by the International Labour Organization—an arm of the United Nations—compared workers in different countries. It found that Americans put in more hours a year than workers in the countries of Europe that had similar economies. Americans worked as much as two weeks more a year than workers in some countries—and as much as five weeks more than Germans.

Repetitive stress injuries can be caused by repeating the same motions over and over again. These kinds of injuries have been more common in the computer age. Many companies have started companywide breaks to allow workers, such as these at Chevron Corporation in Houston, Texas, to stretch their limbs and muscles. (Courtesy of Chevron Corporation)

In addition, the speed of work—and the increasing demands on workers—led to a new phenomenon. It was called "multitasking," and it came from a term for the computer's ability to run more than one program at a time. Workers became accustomed to writing e-mails to one set of people while they talked on the phone to someone else. Some observers warned that multitasking was not a great idea since people who did more than one thing at a time were inefficient or sloppy in their work. American workers were feeling higher levels of stress than in the past.

The Changing Structure of Work

Changes in how work was organized created more stress. In the 1970s and 1980s, Japanese companies were riding a wave of success. Japanese automakers saw their sales soar. Electronics companies made billions by selling high-quality televisions,

To promote company spirit and a sense of community, many employers have begun programs that allow workers and their families to spend time together outside of work. One example is Tom's of Maine, a manufacturer of all-natural toothpaste. The company runs a River Awareness Week, in which employees and their families work together to clean a local river—on company time. (Courtesy of Tom's of Maine)

videocassette players and records, and CD players. Many American business leaders decided that the secret to making their companies successful once again was to do what the Japanese companies did. The result produced radical changes in the way Americans worked.

Some changes involved trying to encourage a feeling of company spirit among workers. Japanese workers identified deeply with their employers. Many began their workdays with mass meetings in which they chanted company slogans or exercised together. Many skeptics said these steps would never work with American workers, who were more interested in being individuals than in identifying with a company. But when Japanese companies opened operations in the United States, they successfully brought in some of these techniques. Some American companies adopted them as well. They found that American workers were indeed willing to show company spirit.

Many manufacturing companies changed the way they made goods. Some dropped the old assembly-line method of having each worker specialize in doing the same task over and over again. Instead, they formed teams who worked together to assemble an entire product. In car factories, then, workers no longer just attached door panels all day long. They became part of a group that put together an entire car. The goal of working in teams was to improve the quality of American products. Teams were thought to make workers more involved in their work. As a result, they would be more satisfied with their work—and more committed to doing the job right.

The movement for quality led to another set of changes. In the old factory system, workers made a product. Later, it was inspected to make sure it met quality standards. If not, it was rejected. The system had a basic flaw. A lot of materials and a lot of time were involved in making, say, a computer. If it was only tested and rejected after all the work was complete, all those materials and all that time—and all the money spent on them—

were simply wasted. New approaches built in quality checkpoints earlier and more often. More important, individual workers were given the authority to halt manufacturing if they saw a major quality problem.

In the past, companies were structured like a pyramid, with a mass of workers reporting to a large number of supervisors. They, in turn, reported to a smaller number of lower-level managers, who reported to even fewer middle managers, who were under a handful of top managers, who reported to the company's chief executive officer (CEO). As the pace of business quickened, circumstances could change rapidly. By the time decisions reached the bottom, the situation might be completely different—and require a different decision.

Business consultant Tom Peters put the issue starkly: "a company cannot survive," he said, "in a time-competitive world with a six- to eight-layer organization structure." The solution was to create a flatter organization, one with fewer levels of managers. Along with that, workers at each level needed to have the power to make decisions about the work that they did.

The new approach was supposed to help the company in many ways. Workers could make decisions more quickly by avoiding the layers of managers. They could respond to situations as they arose and deal with them effectively. They would come to see themselves as entrepreneurs—as people who could intelligently take risks when they saw a chance to help the company make more money. As a result, the company would be more competitive—and more successful. And, as with working in teams, the change would make workers more involved in their work and more satisfied with their jobs.

Another change was to adopt the "just-in-time" system. This change started out in manufacturing but then spread to other kinds of business. Businesses that make goods have to spend money to buy the supplies and materials they need. In the past, they would buy enough to manufacture the product they expected to make in a year. But if sales were slow, and the factory was shut down for a while, those supplies and materials would be just sitting in the factory. That meant money had been spent for no reason. In the new system, companies bought much less material at a time. They might order only enough to cover a month's worth of production. They could then watch how sales were going and, if needed, hold back from buying more goods for the next month. Or if sales were booming, they could step up production by ordering more. The materials would arrive "just in time" for the workers to use them to make the company's product.

Stores began to adopt the "just-in-time" system as well. Instead of ordering large quantities of goods far in advance, they began to order smaller amounts. The new system worked well with the new point-of-sale machines that kept a constant count of the store's inventory of each item on sale. Stores benefited in another way, too. They could carefully watch which items were selling the most and order more of them, skipping styles that were not popular that year.

For some workers, work was organized more flexibly. For most of the 1900s, all workers in a company followed the same schedule, typically 9:00 to 5:00 for office workers. In the late 1900s, many companies began to accept different arrangements. Some adopted "flextime," in which workers could vary the time they arrived or left the office. Typically, companies required employees to be on hand for certain core hours—10:00 in the morning until 4:00 in the afternoon. But workers could work 8:00 to 4:00 or 10:00 to 6:00 if they preferred. This change helped many people fit work better into their lives. Working parents, for instance, could start and leave early so they could be at

During the 1990s a growing number of Americans began to work out of their homes. (Stockbyte Photos)

home when children returned from school. One Department of Labor study showed that as many as a quarter of all workers had some kind of flexibility in their work hours. Another new arrangement was job sharing. In this plan, two people combined to do the job of one worker. They might each work certain hours each day, or they might split the week in half.

A growing number of workers worked at home. Some were full-time employees who simply had home offices. Sales people far from company headquarters, for instance, spent much of their time on the road. When not traveling, they might handle paperwork and correspondence in a home office. With all the new technologies, communication was easy for them. Most home workers, though, worked on their own. Nearly 6 percent of the American workforce made up this category by the late 1900s. They worked in a range of tasks, from consulting to editorial work.

A Worried Workforce

Many of these changes created a worried workforce. Workers had to contend with several pressures. The new technologies forced them to learn new skills. Those who had difficulty mastering computers or other new technologies were left behind. The new ways that companies were organized gave workers more responsibility—but that also created more pressure for them to perform. The increasingly competitive nature of business made companies unwilling to keep employees who were not productive. Many workers felt insecure.

Indeed, many were losing their jobs. Many companies cut jobs to cut costs, a practice called "downsizing" so it would not sound so painful. Corporate mergers often produced a round of layoffs. Sometimes the jolt of losing a job was made worse by heavy-handed actions. Some companies told laid-off workers to pack up their personal belongings and leave that day. Some workers were kept on for a time—so they could train the people who were going to replace them.

Not all workers were treated so harshly. Many companies gave workers help in finding a new job. Many paid the laid-off workers a few months of pay, to tide them over until they found another job. Still, workers who were laid-off typically suffered financially. The Department of Labor found that only about 35 percent—only one in three—found a new job that paid as much as or more than the job they had lost. The vast majority had to take a pay cut.

Even workers who stayed with the company suffered from downsizing. First, they worried that they would be the ones to be let go. Second, they lost friends and fellow workers, often of many years. Third, they faced increased demands on the job. Someone, after all, had to do the work of the people who were let go. Often another worker had to take on new tasks. Workers grumbled at the added workload. Afraid that the company might lay off more workers, they often did not complain too loudly.

In some cases, companies did not pass the work on to staff still employed. Instead, they "out-sourced" the tasks to other companies. This strategy was chosen as part of companies' cost-cutting. It was expensive to train full-time employees and pay their fringe benefits like vacations and health insurance. It could be cheaper to hire an outside firm and pass that responsibility to a smaller company with fewer benefits. Indeed, some laid-off workers went to work for these smaller companies. Sometimes, though, they could only find work with temporary agencies. These groups supplied workers to larger firms on a short-term basis, such as when an employee was on vacation. "Temps," as the replacement workers were called, did not have an easy time. Work was not guaranteed, and wages were typically low. And these workers rarely had benefits like health insurance.

Shrinking Unions

Labor unions might have been able to make the situation easier for America's worried workers. But unions were having problems of their own. The proportion of the workforce that belonged to a union fell sharply throughout the period. In 1960, nearly one out of every three workers was unionized. By 1999, the ratio was closer to one in seven.

There were several reasons for this decline in union membership. One was the change in the workplace. There were fewer manufacturing jobs, where unions were traditionally stronger. And many companies moved factories away from the unionized northern and Midwestern states to the South. Southern states had lower wages and laws that made it more difficult for workers to organize unions. Most new jobs were in service industries, such as retail or in office work. These jobs were not unionized.

Leading American Unions, 2000

LARGEST UNIONS	UNION MEMBERS
National Education Association	2,500,000
International Brotherhood of Teamsters	1,500,000
Service Employees International Union	1,400,000
Food and Commercial Workers International Union	1,400,000
American Federation of State, County, and Municipal Employees	1,300,000
American Federation of Teachers	1,000,000
Laborers' International Union of North America	800,000
International Association of Machinists and Aerospace Workers	780,000
United Automobile, Aerospace & Agricultural Implement Workers International Union	746,000
United Steelworkers of America	700,000
Communications Workers of America	630,000
United Brotherhood of Carpenters and Joiners of America	525,000
American Postal Workers Union	350,000
Hotel Employees and Restaurant Employees	350,000
National Association of Letter Carriers	313,000

Source: World Almanac 2001

Some white-collar workers were unionized, though. They became an increasingly important force in the labor movement. In the past, blue-collar workers—factory workers, construction workers, miners, and truck drivers—had dominated unions. By the late 1900s, some of the largest unions included such white-collar workers as teachers and government employees.

Still, unions were less active in the 1980s and 1990s than in earlier periods. There were fewer strikes each year in these decades than in the 1970s, for instance. Those strikes involved fewer workers. And there were fewer work days lost as a result of strikes.

There were some significant strikes. The first came in 1981, just months after Republican Ronald Reagan became president. In August, Professional Air Traffic Controllers' Association (PATCO), the union for the nation's air-traffic controllers went on strike. These workers controlled the take-offs and landings of passenger jets and used radar to track planes in flight to make sure there were no collisions. They had high-stress jobs, made even worse by huge increases in the amount of air traffic. But the PATCO workers were government employees, and a law banned strikes by such workers. Reagan quoted former President Calvin Coolidge, who had once declared "There is no right to strike against the public safety by anybody, anywhere, at any time." Reagan ordered the controllers back to work in two days. When they refused to return, he fired them all.

Two of the most publicized strikes involved a small group of highly paid workers. They certainly were not traditional blue-collar workers. They were major-league athletes. One of their chief goals was to gain a larger share of the billions of dollars flowing into teams from television revenues and other sources. The players of the National Football League struck in 1981. The players won some rights from the owners in the new contract that followed. Six years later, though, the owners won. The players struck again in 1987, and the owners hired replacement players. After a few games with these replacements, the regular players agreed to return to work. A few years later, the owners put in place a salary cap—a spending limit for each team. The move helped them gain control over the rising cost of player contracts.

Baseball players were more successful. In the late 1970s, players had won the right to become free agents. That is, after a certain number of years with one team, they could sell their services to the highest bidder. Once the right was won, team owners consistently tried to strip it away. The players struck in 1981 for six weeks and in 1985 for a few days. Both times, they kept the upper hand.

In 1994, baseball owners threatened to put in place a salary cap like the one used in football. The players—adamantly opposed to the idea—went on strike in mid-August. The strike lasted through the end of the season, and the World Series was cancelled for the first time in history. The strike dragged into the beginning of the following season. Finally, the owners had to back down, and the players returned to the fields. The players had won again—but at a high cost. When the 1995 season finally began, millions of embittered fans stayed away. Attendance did not reach pre-strike levels for the rest of the decade. In a time when many American workers were worried about their own jobs, they were less willing to support millionaire ballplayers.

Chapter Six

Religion

During the 1980s and 1990s, Americans practiced a growing number of religious faiths. Most people continued to belong to the Roman Catholic and various Protestant churches. Still, religions such as Islam, Buddhism, and Hinduism became increasingly common as new immigrants from Asia arrived in the United States. At the same time, teachings of some well-established faiths found new followers through interest in such traditions as fundamentalism and Kaballah. Some Americans sought out nontraditional religions as well. The result was increasing diversity in American religious life.

South Presbyterian Church (LEFT) **in Dobbs Ferry, New York.** (Jim Burmester/MPI Archives) **Muslims praying** (RIGHT) **inside a Chicago mosque.** (© Ralf-Finn Hestoft/CORBIS SABA)

Continuity and Change

In some ways, religious life in the United States in the late twentieth century was similar to that in earlier times. Gallup poll results concerning religion through the century remained the same on many central issues. In 1947, 95 percent of Americans believed in God. At the end of the century, 96 percent did. About 90 percent of Americans prayed both in 1947 and in the late 1990s. Just over 70 percent believed in life after death at both times. Sixty percent of Americans said that religion was "very important" in their lives in both the late 1960s and the late 1990s.

Yet during the 1980s and 1990s, American spiritual life underwent major changes. One was a drop in church attendance.

About 40 percent of all people said they went to church at the end of the 1990s. The figure had been nearly 50 percent in 1958. Another change was the growth in the number of people who did not belong to a Christian church or who followed new forms of Christian worship.

Although most Americans accepted their fellow citizens' freedom of worship without incident, there were some individuals that committed hate crimes against members of a religion different from theirs. A wave of fire attacks on African American churches took place the late 1980s and early 1990s. Some attacks targeted Muslims, especially in the wake of terrorist attacks on Americans. Early reports of the 1995 bombing of the federal office building in Oklahoma City linked the attack—incorrectly—to Muslims. In the next few days, Muslim people, homes, and places of worship suffered more than 200 attacks. A more frequent target of hate crimes, though, was Jews. Of more than 1,400 hate crimes aimed at religious groups in 1999, only 32 were anti-Islamic while nearly 80 percent were aimed at Jews. Still, the number of these attacks was smaller than earlier in the century.

Christianity

Mainstream Protestant churches struggled in the late 1900s. This group includes Baptist, Methodist, Lutheran, Presbyterian, Episcopalian, and Reformed churches. Nearly 60 percent of all Americans identified themselves as Protestants. But this was a drop from nearly 70 percent in 1947. Many Protestant churches were losing members.

Some denominations that had historically been split into smaller groups re-merged in order to retain members. Three Lutheran churches merged in 1988, uniting nearly 5 million members. Two different Presbyterian groups also joined in the 1980s. This merger brought together northern and southern branches that had split over the issue of slavery in the 1830s. Not all churches could bridge these gaps, however. Baptists remained split into many different groups. Even the Southern Baptist Convention, the largest one, was itself deeply divided on some issues.

Whether to let women and homosexuals become priests or ministers divided many churches. The issue of women priests split some American Catholics from the church leaders in Rome. The

Episcopal church had allowed women to become priests in 1976. In 1988, Barbara Harris became the first woman named as a bishop in that church. In the late 1990s, the Presbyterians, who ordained women, decided not to let homosexuals serve in the clergy. Whether to allow homosexuals to marry was another hot issue. Clergy sometimes carried out commitment ceremonies between homosexuals during these years. Some were punished by church leaders for doing so.

While most Americans were Protestant, the single largest faith was the Roman Catholic Church. More than 60 million people were members. Catholics also were among the most religiously active of all Americans. More than half went to church each week, higher than the national average.

American Catholics had high regard for Pope John Paul II, who had taken office in 1978 and served past the end of the century. The Polish pope won wide support for his strong words against communism and for human freedom. But the pope took many stands that large numbers of American Catholics found difficult. Many American Catholics accepted birth control and abortion, which he condemned. Many were willing to have women in the clergy, which the pope rejected. Many thought that divorced Catholics should be allowed to remarry in the church, which he

Pope John Paul II is broadcast on a large screen while he celebrates mass at the Meadowlands Sports Complex in East Rutherford, New Jersey in 1995. (CORBIS)

would not permit. Catholics responded to this problem in different ways. Some protested church policies. Many made personal decisions based on their own sense of what was right, focusing their religious lives on their local churches and ignoring the pope's positions.

Mormons, members of the Church of Jesus Christ of Latter-Day Saints, numbered nearly 5 million people by the end of the twentieth century. They made a vigorous effort to recruit new members in other countries. Doing much of that work were young men between the ages of eighteen and twenty. They were urged to undertake missionary work for a year or so, even interrupting their education or career plans to do so. The Mormon church thrived in this period. Still, it drew criticism for the facts that it did little to recruit African Americans and that the few black members did not reach leadership posts.

Another significant Christian group was the Eastern Orthodox church. More than 4 million people belonged to the different orthodox churches. These churches trace their origins back to Greek, Russian, and other Christian churches that formed centuries ago. The largest American orthodox church, the Greek Orthodox Archdiocese, went through difficulties in the late 1990s. Members of the church, and many priests, disagreed strongly with Archbishop Spyridon, its top leader. He finally stepped down in favor of a widely respected successor. The church still faced another issue, though. Some members wanted to switch the language of services from traditional Greek to English, which others objected to.

Born-Again and Fundamentalist Christians

A large number of Christians were evangelicals, who felt that they had a close personal relationship with God. They were also called "born-again" Christians because they believed that they received a second birth—a spiritual one—when they had an intense religious experience. Throughout the 1980s and 1990s, from 33 to 40 percent of all Americans considered themselves evangelical Christians. They felt a duty to carry their faith to others.

Some evangelicals practiced their faith within a traditional kind of church. Indeed, by the late 1990s, more than 20 percent of all Catholics called themselves born again. But many formed or joined newer churches. Some met in small Bible study groups. Some of these grew over time until they were large enough to form new congregations with their own buildings. Other evangelicals joined massive "mega-churches." These were 400 or so churches across the country that had more than 2,000 members. One of the earliest mega-churches was the Willow Creek Community Church in Illinois, which drew up to 20,000 people to weekend services. Robert Schuller's Crystal Cathedral, in Southern California, held nearly 3,000 people at a time. More than three times as many could attend Potter's House, an African American church in Dallas, Texas.

Another strong movement in Protestant churches was fundamentalism. Fundamentalists believe that every word in the Old and New Testaments is literally true. They also believe that Jesus will return to Earth to gather believers, a doctrine known as the Second Coming. Fundamentalists and evangelicals share some beliefs, but they differ, too. Evangelicals are more likely to come from mainstream churches. They are also more willing to work with people from other churches. Fundamentalists are more critical of modern culture than evangelicals and more politically active.

One target for this activity in the late 1900s was education. Fundamentalists wanted schools to set aside time for children to pray each day. They led efforts to block teaching children about sex and birth control. They challenged textbooks that reflected what they called "secular humanism," a philosophy that rejects religious faith in favor of values stemming from human reasoning. This view, they said, blurred the lines between right and wrong, and it harmed children. They also attacked the teaching of evolution. This scientific theory about how life developed on Earth was accepted by almost all biologists. But fundamentalists said it denied Bible teaching that God had created the world and formed humans in his own image. Their challenge of teaching this theory back in the 1920s resulted in the famous Scopes trial. In the late 1900s, they attacked it once more, but the effort failed. The Supreme Court ruled that state laws banning the teaching of evolution violated the constitutional separation of church and state. It also struck down state laws that required schools to teach creationism, a theory that tried to use scientific evidence to prove that God had created the world. Convinced that the teaching of evolution was dangerous, many Fundamentalists removed their

Scandals in the Pulpit

Jerry Falwell and Pat Robertson used their television fame to further their political goals. Other preachers focused on religious messages. These televangelists, as they were called, reached audiences numbering millions. Then, late in the 1980s, two scandals rocked religious television. In 1987, preacher Jim Bakker had to resign from his ministry when it became known that he had a longtime affair outside his marriage. Later he was found guilty of fraud for the way he used the money raised through his show. In 1988, preacher Jimmy Swaggart lost his ministry over another scandalous affair. Despite these events, other televangelists continued preaching. Oral Roberts, Robert Schuller, and others kept preaching their messages of faith in God and in the Bible.

children from public schools. Some placed them in private schools that followed Fundamentalist ideas. Others taught their children at home.

Fundamentalists had an impact outside the schools as well. Some fundamentalist leaders became very influential in politics. Jerry Falwell used his recognition as host of a religious television show to form a group called "the Moral Majority" to push for conservative religious and political goals. It created "moral report cards" on members of Congress, rating their support of key issues, such as abortion, school prayer, and homosexual rights. The group campaigned actively for Ronald Reagan's 1980 run for the presidency. It helped conservatives register to vote. It also worked hard to encourage people to vote against candidates who were more liberal.

The Moral Majority faded in just a few years. But the era of fundamentalist activity in politics did not end. The next leader of the Christian Right was Pat Robertson. He, too, had a religious show on television, The *700 Club*. In 1988 Robertson tried to win the Republican nomination for president. Though that effort failed, Robertson continued to be involved in politics.

Judaism

About 5.5 million Jews lived in the United States by the end of the twentieth century. That made them the single largest Jewish population in the world. Their religion mirrored the diversity in American religious life in general. There were three main groups—Orthodox, Conservative, and Reform—and many smaller ones as well. In some ways, Jews were less religious than Protestants or Catholics. Less than a quarter told a Gallup poll that religion was "very important" to them. Just over a quarter attended religious services regularly. But American Jews also had a strong sense of common history and a strong desire to pass on their traditions. Nearly 80 percent of Jewish children received religious teaching.

Tensions divided Jews on some issues. The Reform movement had been, over the years, more open to change. In the late 1900s, some Orthodox leaders began pushing for stricter adherence to several traditional beliefs and practices. This caused anger among some Reform Jews, who felt that their faith was being questioned.

At the same time, Reform Jews wrestled with issues within their movement. A 1990 survey found that nearly two-thirds of the Reform Jews who had married in the previous five years had married someone who was not Jewish. Many Reform congregations wanted their rabbis—the Jewish clergy—to preside over these weddings. Doing so broke a 1973 rule of the Reform church. At the same time, the church adopted a rule in 1983 that recognized the impact of the rise in intermarriages. That year, it officially agreed to define as Jewish a person who had a Jewish father or mother and who was educated in the faith. This broke a very long tradition in which Jewishness was traced through the mother only.

The late 1900s also saw some splits among American Jews on the issue of relations with Israel. Ever since Israel's founding in 1948, American Jews supported the Jewish state. This support intensified from 1967 to the early 1970s, when Israel's existence was threatened by two wars with its Muslim neighbors. American Jews sent financial aid to Israel and backed the American government support for that nation. In the late 1900s, though, some saw certain actions by Israel's government as blocking, rather than promoting, peace with its neighbors. When they voiced criticism of Israel, other American Jews criticized them for undermining the Jewish state. The debate grew heated as peace efforts stalled.

A small but vocal group of American Jews were the followers of Hasidism. This branch of Judaism differs from the traditional focus on teaching by rabbis, emphasizing instead a close personal relationship to God. Beliefs focus on the importance of purity and worship that produces feelings of joy. About 200,000 of the world's 250,000 Hasidic Jews lived in the United States, half of them in New York State. The small Hasidic movement was splintered into several groups, some of whom did not get along well.

A growing movement was the Kabbalah. This very old tradi-

Hasidic Jews dance at a celebration
(© Wally McNamee/CORBIS)

tion emphasized the desire to understand secret messages placed by God in the Torah, the Hebrew scriptures. Kabbalah teachings had special appeal to young people. Many followers of Kabbalah were Christians, which dismayed some Jewish leaders. They feared that the Kabbalah was being pushed away from its roots.

Islam

By the end of the twentieth century, there were about 6 million American Muslims—more than American Jews. That number was going up, as Islam was the fastest growing religion in the country. About 20,000 Americans became Muslims every year. Nearly two-thirds of these converts were African American. In all, about a quarter of all Muslims in the United States—nearly 1.5 million people—were African Americans. One reason for this growth was the increase in immigration from Asia and Africa in recent decades. Only about a quarter of all American Muslims came from the Middle East. About a third were from South Asia.

The nation had about 2,000 mosques, or Muslim places of worship. Unlike Catholicism, where the church is headed by the pope, Islam has no central figure at its head. In the United States, most mosques were locally organized and run. The imam, or religious leader, put his personal stamp on the mosque. Some were traditional. Others were more open to adapting to modern Western ways. Islam reflects another division as well. More than three-quarters of all Muslims are Sunnis. Another 20 percent or so are Shi'ites. The two groups share many beliefs but also differ on some issues, such as the role of religious leaders.

Adapting to American life has been difficult for many Muslims who have come from other lands. Like other immigrant groups, they have seen differences arise between parents and children, who have adapted to American culture and rejected some Muslim traditions. Some adult Muslims also felt clashes between practices common in the United States and Muslim beliefs. For instance, American clothing styles were much less modest than Muslims preferred. The ease with which alcohol could be purchased was a similar problem, as Islam forbids drinking.

Another area of tension is the position of women. Muslims have traditionally not given women rights equal to men. Some Muslims believe that these practices are based on the Quran, Islam's sacred book. They insist that the differences must always be followed. These practices can come into conflict with the position of women in mainstream American culture. Others argue that these practices grew out of Islamic culture and are not central to the religion itself. They are more willing to give women a larger role in Muslim life.

Some Muslims faced problems at work. Muslim women were sometimes refused work because they choose to wear the hijab, or scarf that covers their head. Some Muslim men were punished for insisting on wearing beards. Over time, though, many employers moved to meet the needs of their Muslim workers.

An Islamic mosque
near Toledo, Ohio
(CORBIS)

Many companies allowed workers to take time off for Muslim religious holidays—just as Jewish and Christian workers were allowed time off for theirs—and gave them time for Friday prayers as well.

Another worry for Muslims was their safety. Though hate crimes were relatiavely few, stories about Islamic terrorist attacks on Americans always raised tensions. Many Muslims began to work to spread more information about their religion to other Americans. Others joined groups that became more politically active and campaigned for tolerance and fairer treatment of Muslims in news stories.

Eastern Religions

Harvard Professor Diana Eck studied religion in the United States for many years. Her book *A New Religious America* revealed an important change in American religious life. "The United States," she wrote, "is the most religiously diverse nation in the world." Eck described what the new American religious landscape looked like:

A great Hindu temple with elephants carved in relief at the doorway stands on a hillside in the western suburbs of Nashville, Tennessee. A Cambodian Buddhist temple and monastery with a hint of a Southeast Asian roofline is set in the farmlands south of Minneapolis, Minnesota. In suburban Fremont, California, flags fly from the golden domes of a new Sikh gurdwara.

In the late twentieth century, the country had more diversity in religion than ever before.

The growth in immigrants from countries outside Europe was a major contributor to this diversity. In 1900, Asians accounted for only about 1 percent of all the foreign-born people living in the United States. By 1990, they were about a quarter of all foreign-born people in the United States. They increased the number

Members of Asian Religions in the United States

FAITH	ESTIMATED NUMBER
Ba'hai	140,000
Buddhism	2,450,000
Hinduism	1,200,000
Islam	6,000,000
Jainism	60,000
Sikhism	234,000
Zoroastrianism	18,000

Source: Pluralism Project
www.pluralism.org/resources/statistics/tradition.php

A statue of Buddha in San Francsico's Golden Gate Park (© Reinhard Eisele/CORBIS)

of people who followed Eastern religions. The table on page 98 estimates the number of Americans who belonged to several of these religions in the late 1990s. Some of these groups outnumbered faiths that had long histories in the United States. There were more Buddhists than there were Episcopalians and more Sikhs than Unitarian-Universalists.

Some of these Asian religions had been practiced in the United States for many years. Most of about 25,000 Japanese in the United States in 1900 were Buddhists. About 5,000 Sikhs lived in California at the same time. Also, not all the Asians who came to the United States followed these religions. Some were Christians. Finally, the followers of these religions were not all Asians. As many as 800,000 Buddhists—about a third of the total—were European Americans. Still, there is no question that increased immigration from Asia contributed greatly to the rise in these religions.

As with Christianity, Judaism, and Islam, Buddhism is a diverse religion. There are many different schools of Buddhist belief. This variety was reflected in the United States. In the late 1900s, there was also a distinction among American Buddhists between two main groups. Asian Americans who had a long Buddhist heritage generally followed a style of worship centered on the temple and including weekly services and religious education for children. Among many converts, practice was somewhat different. They tended to focus on types of Buddhism that put more emphasis on meditation. This is the controlled, concentrated breathing that aims to help a person reach a higher state of awareness. One area in which Buddhism has been affected by American culture is growing participation by women.

Hinduism, too, is a diverse religion, with many gods and goddesses and differing styles of worship in northern and southern India. These differences sometimes raised issues among American Hindus. Immigrants from different regions of India or people who tend to worship different gods sometimes had to come together to build temples. They had to find ways to accommodate each other's traditions to create a structure that could meet the religious needs of many. Hindus also had to adapt to American life. The Hindu religious calendar does not match the American work week. Unable to take off work, many Hindus celebrated religious holy days on the nearest weekend, rather than on the exact day.

Nontraditional Religions and Groups

Many smaller groups helped shape religious life in the United States as well. They added to the picture of religious diversity in America. Some were so small that they were unknown—until they were struck by scandal or disaster.

The Church of Scientology was a modern religious movement that drew from ideas in psychology and interest in space travel. It was one of the most controversial of these small groups. The church suffered the death of its founder, L. Ron Hubbard, in 1986, but new leaders carried on the group's work. They met several difficulties, including criticism and investigations by government agencies. A major controversy erupted when one member, who had been ill, died under the care of Scientologists. The dead woman's family sued the church for failing to give her proper medical care. Criminal charges were brought. Though they were later dropped, the lawsuit remained unsettled.

The Wicca movement drew on roots that were far older than Scientology. Also called the Craft or Neo-Paganism, the Wicca movement is the practice of witchcraft. The movement was very diverse. There were two main groups, but there are also many individuals who built their own set of beliefs. The exact number of Wiccans was unclear. Some experts said that there were as many as 750,000.

Another movement that drew from old ideas was the New Age movement. It combined the ideas of nineteenth-century European thinkers with Asian religions. The movement also mixed in other traditional ideas. For instance, it included astrology, the belief that a person's character and life is shaped by the planets. Astrology gave the movement its name—and its hopeful view of the future. Astrologers believed that the world was entering a new age that would bring world peace and spiritual harmony. Some believers thought the change would take place on a particular day in 1987. Thousands gathered at sacred spots around the world in the hopes that their spiritual energy would help transform the world. When the changes failed to follow, many lost faith. Still, the movement left its mark. Many people felt that they had won a greater spiritual understanding through what they had learned.

Two small religious groups ended in disaster. One was Heaven's Gate, which combined traditional Christian teaching with some Asian influences. A key belief was that aliens from another planet had come to earth and would return. Believers held that they would lose their bodies and be taken into a spaceship sent by the aliens. Then they would be transported to another world to enjoy a more spiritual life. Followers believed that the Hale-Bopp comet that appeared in 1997 would bring the spaceship. In preparation for their journey, all 39 members killed themselves.

The Branch Davidians also ended in death. Founded back in 1929, the group came under the control of a new leader, David Koresh, in 1990. His stated goal was to carry out acts described in the biblical Book of Revelations, which would produce the Second Coming of Jesus and cause the end of the world. The group began to gather food and weapons to bear them through the terrible time. Some people who had left the group raised alarms. They claimed that Koresh and others had committed child abuse at the group's compound at Waco, Texas.

In late February 1993, federal law enforcement agents showed up at the compound. They hoped to investigate charges that the group had illegal guns, but a shootout resulted. Six Davidians and four federal agents were killed, and many more were wounded. The Federal Bureau of Investigation (FBI) then surrounded the compound, locking members inside in a standoff that lasted more than 50 days. When negotiations to end it failed, the FBI decided to attack. On April 19, 1993, it sent tear gas inside the Davidians' building, hoping to disable those inside. But the plan went horribly wrong. Fires broke out inside. There were also gunshots. In the end, 76 Davidians died, including Koresh and 21 children. Only eight members escaped.

Attorney General Janet Reno faced withering criticism for her decision to use force. Though several investigations cleared the FBI of doing anything wrong, anger lingered. Some extreme conservatives saw the Waco raid as an example of the government's plan to rob people of their rights. One of these extremists was Timothy McVeigh. On April 19, 1995—exactly two years after the Waco attack—he used a truck bomb to blow away the front of a government office building in Oklahoma City. One hundred sixty-eight people died.

Summary

By the end of the twentieth century, American religious life looked similar to that of earlier times—and also quite different. Huge majorities of Americans believed in God and prayed. The United States—always a deeply religious nation—remained so even in a secular, or worldly, age. Even though the United States was generally a wealthy society with many material comforts, then, people still had deep spiritual needs. Many Americans turned to religion to recover from these emotional and spiritual blows of fast-paced modern life and its economic and personal pressures.

Religion in America—always very diverse—had grown even more varied. New religions became more prominent than they had been, and immigrant groups tried to find ways to adapt their religious beliefs to the rhythms and customs of American culture. Several Christian churches underwent changes as people sought new ways to understand the world. Yet the absence of large numbers of attacks by one set of believers on another confirmed that freedom of religion was firmly planted in American culture. The acceptance of many different religions was shown forcefully by the armed forces. By the late 1990s, the navy had a mosque for Muslim sailors serving at the Norfolk Naval Base, and Wiccan leaders held services each week for Wiccan soldiers.

Chapter Seven

Health, Science, and Technology

Science and technology passed many milestones in the twentieth century. Many predictions had been made throughout the century of the marvels that humans would enjoy in the year 2000. While flying cars never appeared, there were still plenty of discoveries and advances in the 1980s and 1990s. Science and technology made life in 1999 very different from what it had been in 1960—let alone in 1900.

Leading Technologies

Four technologies came into wide use in the 1980s and 1990s. First was the personal computer. PCs revolutionized how work was done (see Chapter 5). They also changed how people spent their free time, after reaching to nearly half of all American homes by the late 1990s. One reason for this spread was the growth of Internet use. The Internet had been launched in the 1970s as a way of linking computers in defense research. It became much more widespread in 1990 when the World Wide Web was born. This new use of the Internet allowed people or companies to display images, sounds, and moving pictures as well as text. Very quickly, companies began to sell goods and services over the Web.

In 1987, a giant quilt commemorating victims of AIDS was displayed at a ceremony (LEFT) at the National Mall in Washington, DC. (© Susan Steinkamp/ CORBIS) **The U.S. Space Camp in Huntsville, Alabama offers campers a chance to test equipment used by real astronauts. This young man (RIGHT) operates a machine called a remote arm.** (National Aeronautics and Space Administration)

The "Y2K Bug"

Trouble lurked inside the programs that computers ran. For many years, most programs had used only the last two digits of a date to indicate the year. They simply dropped the "19" that showed the century. As a new century loomed, fears arose that the computer would read "01" as 1901, not 2001. Authorities warned that insurance and bank records would become full of errors if the programs were not repaired. They said that the nation's electric, water, and food systems might break down. Programmers worked feverishly to fix the problem. The U.S. government and businesses spent $350 billion to fix the "Y2K bug." January 1, 2000, dawned with relatively few problems.

Universities, libraries, and museums began to post information. Interest groups used the Web to push their causes. People quickly moved to tap into this new source of information—and entertainment. By 1999, about a third of all homes had access to the Web, and the number kept growing. The wide use of computers raised a potential problem at the end of the century, though (see sidebar).

The second major technology was the spread of lasers. These devices use mirrors to focus a thin but powerful stream of light. They, too, had their first significant use for defense. The military used lasers to make sure that missiles and planes ran true to course. After the 1980s, they became much more widespread. At home, consumers used lasers in CD players to listen to music. In stores, cashiers used lasers to scan bar codes on product packages or labels to total a customer's bill. In offices, workers used lasers to print reports or make photocopies. Lasers were also used in medicine. They could break up material that clogged arteries, destroy cancerous tumors, and fix vision problems.

Like lasers, fiber optics also had medical uses. Tiny fiber-optic cables could be inserted into a patient's body. Because they were flexible, they could bend to follow the throat or blood vessels. By connecting them to video cameras, doctors could look inside a person's internal organs without making large surgical cuts. Indeed, fiber optics could be used for surgery by attaching special tools to the tubes. Such careful operations did less damage to the patient's body than older methods. That made it easier for patients to recover.

The last important technology came in the field of genetics. This is the study of how living things pass characteristics on from one generation to the next. In the 1950s, scientists found that DNA in cells carried a unique set of codes for each living thing. In the 1970s, they found ways to snip sections of DNA from one place and patch them into another spot. Thus was born the new field of genetic engineering. It is also called biotechnology. Events in 1980 signaled that the new field would be important. That year, two scientists manipulated DNA to create a new drug that could be used to fight cancer.

At first, progress was slow. By the late 1980s, only a few substances produced by these new methods had been patented. Soon after, many new products came out. Some were medicines aimed at fighting various diseases, but many were foods. Scientists created tomatoes that could last longer before they spoiled. They made plants, such as corn, that had built-in resistance to insect pests or plant diseases. They created cows that produced 10 percent more milk than normal cows. Some people viewed these new products with alarm. They worried that foods with altered genes could cause health problems for the people who ate them. Many countries in Europe banned the sale of these foods.

In 1996, another breakthrough grabbed the headlines. Researchers in Scotland announced that they had cloned a sheep. In cloning, scientists use biotechnology to create an exact copy of an animal. Cloning raised many questions, one of which was the high rate of failure. Before scientists made Dolly the cloned sheep, they had failed in more than 270 attempts.

Dolly, the cloned sheep, was born in a Scotland laboratory. (Courtesy of Roslin Institute)

There were deep moral questions as well. Most people agreed that cloning humans was not a good idea, but people were divided about using the same technology to grow healthy organs or skin tissue. These could be stored and used as replacements if a person needed a new heart or a skin graft. That sounded appealing to some, but questions still remained. People were also concerned about who would control the supply of material and whether advances would only be available to the wealthy.

Medical Technology

Lasers and fiber optics were not the only new tools being used in health care in the late twentieth century. Doctors made many other breakthroughs. New machines made it easier to locate and identify problems in the body. Using sound, magnetic, or electric waves, they showed "soft tissues"—the muscles and organs that did not show up on X-rays. These images were more accurate, too. They showed the body in three dimensions. With these tools, doctors could make sure that babies were developing in healthy ways inside their mothers' bodies. They could find areas where the brain was not working properly.

There were also advances in surgery. One new operation was called angioplasty. Doctors inserted tiny tubes into the arteries that bring blood to the heart muscle. The tubes carried balloons that expanded once in place, which forced fat deposits against the artery wall and cleared the artery.

Scientists also found new, more effective ways of treating diseases. While cancer was still a major threat, new treatments worked better than ever before. In 1996, for the first time since statistics had been kept, the rate of death from cancer fell from the previous year. Doctors had much better success in saving the lives of women with breast cancer than ever before. They also had success with other types of cancer, including skin cancer.

A major health crisis arose early in the 1980s when a devas-

Leading Causes of Death

The table compares the leading causes of death in 1900, 1940, and 1998. During this period, infectious diseases like tuberculosis and intestinal diseases dropped off the chart. The lifestyle diseases, however, figure higher in the list of leading causes.

	1900	1940	1998
#1	Pneumonia	Heart disease	Heart disease
#2	Tuberculosis	Cancer	Cancer
#3	Intestinal diseases	Stroke	Stroke
#4	Heart disease	Kidney disease	Lung disease
#5	Stroke	Pneumonia and influenza	Accidents
#6	Liver disease	Accidents, except motor vehicle accidents	Pneumonia and influenza
#7	Accidents	Tuberculosis	Diabetes
#8	Cancer	Diabetes	Suicide
#9	Senility	Motor vehicle accidents	Kidney disease
#10	Diphtheria	Premature birth	Liver disease

Source: National Center for Health Statistics, "DataWarehouse/Historical Data"

tating new disease appeared. This was AIDS (acquired immune deficiency syndrome). The first evidence that something was wrong arose in the late 1970s. Doctors saw some people dying from very rare diseases. They found that these individuals had weakened immune systems—the body system that fights disease. In 1981, the condition was given the name AIDS. Throughout the 1980s, the number of AIDS cases rose at a fast rate. Unfortunately, the great majority of people with the disease died, and the death tolls rose quickly. In 1985, nearly 7,000 people in the United States died of the disease. In 1994, nearly 50,000 people did.

Researchers worked feverishly to find what caused the disease—and how to cure it. Within a few years, they found that the problem was a virus named human immunodeficiency virus (HIV). HIV attacked the body's immune system. As a result, the body could not fight off diseases. Researchers also found that people gave the virus to one another by exchanging blood or other body fluids. Public health officials mounted education campaigns to try to curb the spread. Meanwhile, other researchers worked on finding ways of treating or curing HIV infection. Though they could not find a complete cure, they did develop some powerful medicines. Some drugs stopped the infection from turning into AIDS. Others slowed the rate at which the disease damaged the immune system. By the late 1990s, the rate of infection dropped each year, from more than 76,000 a year in 1994 to less than 50,000 in 1998. The number of deaths fell from nearly 50,000 a year in 1994 to under 14,000 in 1998.

Asthma was another lifestyle disease growing in frequency. In this condition, the airways in a person's lungs become narrow. They do not carry a full supply of oxygen. This leaves a person short of breath—and in an extreme attack can cause death. In the late 1900s, asthma rates rose higher than ever before, reaching as much as 5 percent of the population. Children, in particular, were affected in growing numbers. The causes for this increase were unknown, though air pollution was suspected. Doctors had medicines to treat the condition, but the rising rates were alarming.

Researchers had found many antibiotics that could defeat infectious diseases. But some of the germs that cause those diseases changed over time. They developed the ability to resist the medicines. Doctors had to give the drugs in higher doses to beat the disease. Some experts worried that they would reach a point where the medicines would no longer work.

Environmental Issues

Some older technologies remained important in the late twentieth century. Most of that technology relied on fossil fuels—gasoline, oil, coal, and natural gas. More than 90 percent of all households had at least one car, and those cars burned gasoline. Energy to heat and cool people's homes and to run their many electrical appliances came from fossil fuels. The heavy use of these sources of energy had a great impact on the environment.

One problem was pollution. The burning of fossil fuel produced smoke and chemicals that could poison the air. Congress had passed the Clean Air Act in the 1970s, and much progress was made in cutting down on pollution. But several more serious problems remained. One was acid rain. Some of the chemicals sent into the air came back to earth when rain fell. The chemical-laden water did great harm, killing fish and other life in lakes and trees in forests. The government told power plants to limit the chemicals they released. The crisis became less extreme, but some damage to lakes and forests remained.

Another problem, some scientists said, was the buildup of exhaust gases in the atmosphere. Burning these fuels pumped carbon dioxide into the air. Large amounts were trapped there, and these scientists feared long-term damage would result. They said that the gas would trap warmth near the earth's surface, just as the glass sides and roof of a greenhouse do. This "greenhouse effect" would lead to a warmer climate. If so, the ice caps at the North and South Poles would melt, raising the level of the seas. Higher seas would flood islands and coastal areas. Many of the world's most populous cities were located there. The warmer earth would also lead to climate change. That could hurt the ability to raise enough food for the world's growing population.

Not all scientists agreed. Some dismissed these dire warnings. They pointed out that the world's climate had changed many times before. Still, the idea of global warming gained wide acceptance in 1992. That year, leaders from more than 100 countries met in Rio de Janeiro, Brazil. They discussed ways of cutting down on the emission of the chemicals that produced this effect. The Rio Summit ended with a broad agreement that, by 2000, countries should limit their emissions to the same amount as in

1990, which would help by stopping the growth of these emissions. Some progress was made by the end of the decade, but not as much as had been hoped for at the Rio Summit.

The use of fossil fuels did other damage to the environment. Some methods used to mine coal scarred the land. Leaks from oil pipelines damaged nature as well. There were several accidents in which the ships that carried oil around the world sank, and some caused tremendous damage. The worst such accident in American history took place in 1989. An oil tanker named the *Exxon Valdez* lost control and ran aground off Prince William Sound in Alaska. The rocks ripped holes in the ship's hull, which dumped nearly 11 million gallons of oil into the fragile waters of the sound. Oil slicks washed ashore along hundreds of miles of coast. Thousands of animals died. Even after months of work, the area could not be completely cleaned. Exxon had to pay $100 million in fines. It also had to turn over $5 billion in damages to fishers who could no longer ply their trade.

There was also concern about the limited amount of coal and oil in the Earth. Once all the coal was dug up and all the oil pumped, people wondered what would happen. Dams used the power of water to create electricity. But dams could not meet a

Scientists perform an autopsy on a gray whale which is stranded on the shore of Kodiak Island, Alaska, after the *Exxon Valdez* oil spill, 1989. (© Natalie Fobes/CORBIS)

large share of the country's energy needs. Many parts of the country did not have rivers that could be dammed. Also, scientists realized that damming rivers changed the land in dramatic—and sometimes harmful—ways. Salmon populations in the Northwest suffered because dam projects blocked the rivers where adult fish laid their eggs.

Nuclear energy had once been seen as a replacement for fossil fuels. In the 1950s, many people believed that nuclear power would provide cheap, clean energy. Many nuclear power plants were built, but over the years opposition to them grew. One reason was that used nuclear fuel was radioactive—and very dangerous—for hundreds of years. Hot debates arose over how to safely dispose of plant waste. In fact, citizens often tried to block efforts to move nuclear waste storage facilities in their areas.

This opposition to nuclear power grew even stronger after the 1979 leak at the Three Mile Island nuclear power plant near Harrisburg, Pennsylvania. Though no one was killed, nearby areas were evacuated. Construction of new nuclear plants was halted. Just seven years later, a far more disastrous accident hit the Soviet Union. An explosion in the Chernobyl nuclear plant left several people dead and contaminated a wide area. These accidents increased concern about the safety of nuclear plants. The growth of nuclear power slowed. By 1999, less than 8 percent of energy in the United States was provided by nuclear power. Fossil fuels supplied ten times more.

Work was done to find new sources of energy. Some power companies used the wind to generate electricity. Some people—and companies—used special panels to use energy from the sun to power buildings. By the end of the century, though, less than 10 percent of the nation's energy came from these sources.

A disaster of the late 1970s had convinced many Americans that they might not be safe at home. Love Canal was a community in New York State that had been built near a site where toxic chemicals had been dumped. The chemicals worked their way through the ground into people's homes. There they caused birth defects and other serious health problems. Soon reports emerged of other dangerous sites around the country. In 1980, Congress acted. It passed a law creating the Superfund. This was a sum of money that could be used to clean up these dangerous sites. Efforts were made to carry out the work, and billions of dollars were spent. By the end of the century, though, many sites still remained untouched. Some critics of the cleanup effort said that it was racially biased. It focused on white suburbs and ignored urban neighborhoods that were home to racial minorities.

Probing Space

While debates raged over the condition of the earth's environment, NASA, the National Aeronautics and Space Administration continued exploring space. The vehicles that transported astronauts into space were the space shuttles. The shuttles could be used over and over again—unlike the capsules of the 1960s and early 1970s. Each was shaped like a huge airplane. Propelled into orbit around the Earth by powerful rockets, they returned to land like a glider. Each had a huge cargo bay that could carry satellites and other equipment into space. The first shuttle, *Columbia*, flew in 1981 in a successful test of this new technology.

With *Columbia*'s success, NASA built three more shuttles, and more flights took place. But in January 1986, disaster struck. Barely a minute after takeoff, the shuttle *Challenger* exploded. All seven crew members died. One of them, a teacher named Christa McAuliffe, was to be one of the first civilians to reach space. NASA officials began an investigation that uncovered some embarrassing facts. Engineers had warned the agency of weaknesses in the system that had failed. The pressure to launch had overridden those warnings. Officials vowed to change the way NASA worked to prevent another such disaster. Engineers fixed the mechanical problems. New management systems were put in place to try to ensure the safety of future launches.

Late in 1988, after a delay of two and a half years, shuttle flights resumed. For the next several years, NASA sent up from three to six flights a year. This was fewer than NASA had originally planned. Still, the missions became routine enough that many Americans lost interest in the shuttle

The space shuttle *Challenger* lifts off in 1986. Minutes later, the shuttle exploded, killing everyone aboard. (National Aeronautics and Space Administration)

The Hubble Space Telescope (National Aeronautics and Space Administration)

flights. A 1998 flight marked a milestone. That year, John Glenn—the first American to orbit Earth back in 1963—returned to space. At 77, he became the oldest person to fly in space.

Late in the 1990s, NASA entered a new era. Starting in 1998, shuttle trips focused on creating a new space station. The new structure was called the "International Space Station" because sixteen countries took part in the effort. More than forty shuttle missions would be needed to build the station by the expected completion date of 2005. The first three-person crew moved into the station in the fall of 2000.

In 1990, a shuttle mission put a new telescope into orbit around the earth. The Hubble Space Telescope promised to give scientists views into the universe that humans had never seen before. Since it was outside the Earth's atmosphere, it could see farther than telescopes on the planet's surface. Soon after the Hubble was placed in orbit, though, problems arose. A mirror in the telescope was found to be faulty. Other problems were found as well. In 1993, a space shuttle crew visited the telescope and fixed these problems. Soon after, the telescope began producing stunning images of the universe. One observer said that the instrument was "the most significant single device to scan the skies" since the first telescope 300 years before. The telescope provided useful new information about the size and nature of the universe and the objects in it.

Some of NASA's most important scientific work came from probes, or unmanned vehicles. Two had been launched in the 1970s but did some work in the 1980s. *Voyager 1* reached Saturn in November 1980 and studied that planet. It then continued moving, to become the first human-made vehicle to leave the solar system. *Voyager 2* visited Jupiter and Saturn before continuing to Uranus and Neptune. It, too, left the solar system. The *Global*

Surveyor found signs that Mars had once had water. The *Lunar Prospector* also found evidence of water on the moon.

One of the most spectacular finds from another planet, though, was discovered back on Earth. In 1996, scientists announced that they had found, in Antarctica, a rock that had once been on Mars. The ancient rock had been split off from its home when an asteroid had hit the surface of Mars. A few thousand years ago, a piece landed on Earth. Scientists knew that the rock was from Mars because the gases inside it matched those inside rocks analyzed on Mars itself. The most amazing thing about the rock was that it had evidence that microscopic forms of life had been living on Mars 3.6 billion years ago.

The Shape of Things to Come

Of course, many of the developments described in this chapter did not begin in the 1980s and 1990s. The origins of computers, lasers, and fiber optics could be found years before. The same will be true in the future. Among the many areas of research late in the 1900s, three were particularly promising.

One is nanotechnology, the name given to the process of building machines by putting atoms together. In traditional manufacturing, people shape materials like steel or wood or plastic into the desired form. With nanotechnology, workers start with atoms themselves, assembling them to make microscopic machines. K. Eric Drexler, who coined the term nanotechnology in the 1980s, predicted fabulous results. Nanotechnology, he wrote, will "bring changes as profound as the Industrial Revolution, antibiotics, and nuclear weapons all rolled up into one massive breakthrough." Experts predicted that nanotechnology could be used to make computers and to make devices that could fix damaged cells in the body. It could even be used to create replicators—machines that would make other machines—or make food—simply by putting together atoms in certain ways.

Engineers also worked to make cheap superconductors. These devices move electricity more freely than existing materials. Copper wires carry only 85 percent of the electricity pumped into them. The other 15 percent is simply lost. Superconductors conduct all of this electric power, cutting down the amount of oil or coal that had to be burned. As the century ended, companies were busily working to find materials that would serve.

The Human Genome Project provided the basis for new breakthroughs in medicine. This ambitious effort aimed at understanding the complete DNA code for human beings. Launched in 1990, the effort had a formidable task. To complete the work entirely, scientists would need to examine about 3 billion interlocking pairs of information that make up DNA. Complicating the issue was the fact that only about 5 to 10 percent of human DNA made up the genes that actually control life and health. The rest was more or less background noise—useless information. By 2000, though, two of the chief research labs announced that they had finished the initial mapping work. Much more needed to be done, from analyzing the results to finding ways of using the information. But this work gave researchers tools to locate the specific causes of some health problems and the possibility of identifying new ways for medicines to work more effectively.

Summary

Science and technology transformed life in the late 1900s. Computers became vital tools for work and devices used every day for entertainment, getting information, and communicating. Lasers and fiber optics transformed how business was done and, with advances in genetics, changed health care. Other advances in medicine made it possible to cure diseases far better than ever before in human history, though the appearance of AIDS and rising rates of asthma were worrisome. Some advances were made in caring for the environment. Still, the widespread burning of fossil fuels remained an issue for the future. The space shuttle missions led to new ways of seeing the universe and, in the construction of the International Space Station, set the stage for a permanent human presence outside the Earth. Research into new technology provided the groundwork for other advances to be made in the future.

Chapter Eight

Leisure, Sports, and Entertainment

The worlds of the arts, entertainment, and sports saw many changes in the 1980s and 1990s. There were new technologies that changed methods of artistic expression and vehicles for media culture. CDs and music videos emerged, while videocassettes gained wide popularity. New movements, such as grunge and rap music, arose. New stars rose to the top, including singers, such as Madonna and athletes, such as Michael Jordan who dominated their fields. There was a growing diversity of voices, shown in the rise of new television channels and the spread of independent films, the publishing of works by minority writers, the growing popularity of Latino music, and the rise of new sports and women's sports.

The cast of *Seinfeld* (LEFT), **one of the top television sitcoms of the 1990s** (Darius Anthony/Castle Rock Entertainment)**; actor Larry Hagman** (RIGHT) **played J.R. Ewing on the 1980s drama** *Dallas.* (Movie Star News)

The Rise of Cable TV

The 1980s and 1990s saw hundreds of network shows, from comedies to dramas to news magazines. Some lasted only about a month. Some had considerably more staying power. Probably the biggest hit of the 1980s was *The Cosby Show*, in which Bill Cosby dispensed one-liners and paternal wisdom that provoked laughter and touched the heart. The comedy reigned as the country's top show five years in a row in the late 1980s. Other major comedy hits were *Seinfeld*—standup comic Jerry Seinfeld's "show about nothing"—and the group comedy *Friends*. *The Simpsons*, a snappy satire, began in 1989 and continued well past 2000, making it the longest-running prime-time cartoon show ever.

The top dramas of the 1980s included the prime-time soap operas *Dallas* and *Dynasty*, both about the tangled loves and devious plots of wealthy families. *Dallas* was the nation's most watched show for three years in the early 1980s. People in more than 40 million homes watched a single episode, which revealed who had shot J.R., the conniving main character. Other important dramas included the gritty police shows *Hill Street Blues* and *N.Y.P.D. Blue*. The big winner in the late 1990s was *ER*, which followed the professional and personal difficulties of a group of emergency room doctors and nurses. The quirky *Northern Exposure* and the hip *Ally McBeal* both combined comedy and drama. The *X-Files* became a cult hit by dramatizing an alleged government conspiracy to cover up visits by aliens. A 1960s cult hit, *Star Trek*, returned to television in three spin-off series—each of which ran longer than the original.

The period also saw some famous farewells. The 1970s hit *M.A.S.H* finally shut down after ten years of thoughtful and hilarious scripts. Its final episode, aired in February 1983, was a two-and-a-half hour show. Seen in more than 50 million households, it became the most-watched television event of all time. More than 42 million homes tuned into the final episode of *Cheers* ten years later. *Seinfeld*'s last show was also widely seen.

While some shows attracted huge audiences, the big three networks—ABC, CBS, and NBC—had troubles in the late 1990s. They had dominated television programming from the 1950s to the 1970s. By 1977, more than 90 percent of the people watching television watched one of those three networks. In the next two decades, that completely changed.

One challenge to the big three came from new networks. The first was Fox, launched in 1987 by Australian media tycoon Robert Murdoch. Fox began modestly, broadcasting shows only two nights a week. Those shows were aimed at young, urban viewers, often at African Americans. Over time, Fox built an audience and put more shows on the air. In 1994, it stunned the television world by buying the rights to show National Football League games. The move knocked CBS out of pro football after thirty years. It also signaled that Fox had become a force in the industry. Some local CBS affiliate stations abandoned the old network for the growing Fox. By the late 1990s, Fox had as many affiliates as the big three and was running a full schedule of shows.

Two other independent networks, UPN and WB, followed Fox's lead. Both were launched by giant media companies, and both began slowly but grew over time. Later the Spanish-language networks Univision and Telemundo emerged. Their rise was yet another signal of the growing influence of Latinos in the United States.

The biggest challenge to network power, though, came from cable television. Television signals were first sent over underground cables in the late 1940s. At first, the technology was used mainly to reach rural areas that could not receive a strong broadcast signal through the air. Cable became far more widespread in the later 1900s. Cities and towns across the country sold the rights to companies to put cables in place and offer programming. The new systems spread quickly. In 1980, just under 20 percent of American homes with a television were wired for cable. By 1998, more than 67 percent were.

They could see dozens of channels. Movie fans watched HBO and Showtime. The sports channel, ESPN, offered games and sports talk twenty-four hours a day. The need for more programming led to "narrowcasting." Production companies formed new channels that tried to appeal to small markets that had deep interest in a particular subject. Any time of day or night, viewers could watch golf tournaments—or get helpful tips for improving their game—on the Golf Channel. Or they could learn home improvement methods on Home and Garden. Or they could learn more about the world on the Discovery Channel. By the late 1990s, there were more than 150 different cable channels.

Cable became too powerful for the networks to ignore, and they began to move into cable. In the 1990s, NBC launched two cable channels. ABC and CBS both made programming deals with cable companies. Fox also joined, with its own cable news and entertainment channels.

As a result of these changes, the three network's share of the viewers fell steadily. By 1999, under 50 percent of all televisions were tuned to network shows. Cable itself was commanding about 30 percent of the audience. The rest was split among the three rival networks (Fox, UPN, and WB) and people using their TVs to watch videos.

The loss of network power was evident in news coverage. Shrinking network audiences resulted in lower network revenues. The big three began to close news bureaus, especially overseas. Cable News Network (CNN) jumped in to fill the void. CNN's ambition was to become the world's main source of news. It posted journalists in countries around the world. In 1991, the move paid off. When air strikes in Baghdad, Iraq, signaled the beginning of the Persian Gulf War, CNN cameras caught the explosions—live. Nearly 10 million homes tuned to CNN during the Gulf War. After the war, its audience fell back to prewar levels, but CNN remained a force in news. Indeed, NBC and Fox launched their own round-the-clock news channels.

Another trend was syndication. Local stations needed programs to fill the daytime and early evening hours, when there were no network shows. For much of this programming, they turned to syndicated shows. In syndication, rights to shows are sold individually to local stations across the country. The companies that own the shows collect the fees; the local stations got the programming they needed. Syndicated shows were often reruns of network shows, game shows, and talk shows. Situation comedies like *The Cosby Show*, *Cheers*, *Seinfeld*, and *Friends* continued their broadcast success in years of syndication. The game shows *Jeopardy* and *Wheel of Fortune* became popular in the early evening.

Talk shows were typically daytime fare. The success of pioneers like Phil Donahue encouraged producers to seek more hosts and hostesses who could discuss political, personal, and cultural issues with a range of guests. None proved as appealing—or successful—as Oprah Winfrey. Starting with locally produced talk shows, she was syndicated across the country by the middle 1980s. With a sympathetic manner, probing mind, and great business sense, she gained a huge audience. Guests felt comfortable speaking freely about their ideas and experiences. Audiences were captivated by her calm, reassuring manner. Winfrey became one of the richest and most successful women in the country. She also had great influence. Books she recommended enjoyed a surge in sales. Winfrey's endorsement of Toni Morrison's *Song of*

Solomon turned a nineteen-year-old book into a bestseller. A first-time novelist who appeared on Winfrey's show sold nearly a million copies of her book. Her on-air book club helped build a growing reading public.

The Music Scene

One of the biggest cable winners was MTV—Music Television. Launched in 1981, MTV grew explosively. By the late 1980s, it claimed more than 30 million viewers a week. It made $50 million in profits a year. Young people around the world wanted their own versions of the popular channel. Offerings like MTV Asia, MTV Europe, and MTV Latino boosted the company's reach to more than 250 million homes.

Michael Jackson
(Movie Star News)

The network showed music videos. These slick productions, produced to promote new pop or rock songs, became an art form in themselves. They were not a new technology in the late twentieth century. The Beatles and other groups had made them back in the 1960s. MTV gave a real push to music videos, though. It provided a forum for people to see them. The tight choreography and elaborate productions seen on the videos of Michael Jackson and Madonna helped, too.

These performers were the big music stars of the 1980s. Jackson's *Thriller* album sold an astounding 40 million copies and captured eight Grammy awards. The cross-over appeal of the "King of Pop" also helped change pop music on television. MTV showed few videos from African American artists before *Thriller*. Afterwards, videos by black performers were shown often on MTV. Madonna's controversial videos generated much debate in households across America. She challenged social conventions in crisply choreographed and elaborately produced videos and concerts. Her sales topped $1 billion in less than ten years.

Madonna
(Movie Star News)

Jackson and Madonna appealed to wide audiences. The major trend of the period in music, though, was diversity. Listeners could choose among many different sounds, including rock, pop, heavy metal, salsa, rhythm and blues, rap, Christian rock, country, and more. Four major movements in the music business were grunge, rap, Latino performers, and new forms of country. Grunge was a form of rock that arose in Seattle in the late 1980s and became popular nationally in the 1990s. The main successes to come out of this sound were the bands Nirvana and Pearl Jam. The heavy guitars and strong beat appealed to many teens, who viewed the sound—and the group's heartfelt, troubled lyrics—as more honest than the standard pop music. Nirvana won several awards and legions of fans, but the group faded when lead singer Kurt Cobain killed himself in 1994. Pearl Jam continued to enjoy success at the end of the decade.

Rap debuted in 1979, when the Sugarhill Gang put out "Rapper's Delight." The new music based on poetic rhymes first appealed to black youth in the country's inner cities but quickly spread to white teens in the suburbs. Rapper Eazy-E explained why rap had this appeal. "We're like reporters," he said. "We give [our listeners] the truth. People where we come from hear so many lies that the truth stands out like a sore thumb." Performers like Ice Cube and LL Cool J gained great success. Some aspects of rap raised some worries. One problem was rappers' lack of respect for women, who were often described and treated in rap videos in demeaning ways. Female artists like Queen Latifah voiced musical objections to this trend. Even more troubling to some was the "gangsta rap" movement. Gangsta, which arose in the early 1990s, seemed to celebrate violence. That image was confirmed in the late 1990s, when two gangsta rappers, Tupac Skakur and the Notorious B.I.G., were shot to death. Despite these controversies, rap proved a vibrant and influential new form of music. It gained wide popularity around the world. In 1999, rising star Eminem, a white rapper, took the form in new directions.

Spanish-language music became popular in the United States in the last two decades of the century. There were many different styles of Latino music. Celia Cruz and Tito Puente sang and played salsa. Rising young star Selena made the Tex-Mex sound called "Tejano" music popular until her career was cut short when she was shot to death. Cuban-born Gloria Estefan gave vocals for The Miami Sound Machine, which updated traditional Caribbean sounds. Guitarist Carlos Santana appealed to many with his mix of salsa, rock, and jazz. The European sound of Julio Iglesias charmed many. Whatever the flavor, Latino music gained a wider audience in the late 1990s. This grew in part from the country's rising Latino population. By the end of the decade, Jennifer Lopez had become one of the top sellers of music and had starred in several movies as well.

Unlike rap, country music had been around for decades. Unlike Latino music, it did not come from overseas. It had been born in the hills of Kentucky, the farms of the South, and the ranches of the West. But country music changed profoundly in the late twentieth century. A new generation of country performers fused the traditional sound of country with music influenced by rock. Singer-songwriters like Garth Brooks and Clint Black wrote songs that had a new flavor. By the late 1990s, country music was enjoying great success and gaining new listeners.

Clint Black
(Movie Star News)

The Silver Screen

Movies saw many changes as well. New technologies made it possible for moviemakers to create stunning special effects. *Star Wars* set a new standard in this area when it was released in 1977. Later films reached even more stunning achievements. *E.T.* (1982) had a cuddly alien, though the *Alien* movies (1979, 1986, and 1992) included more threatening space monsters. *Who Framed Roger Rabbit?* (1988) combined live action with cartoon characters in a ground-breaking movie. In the 1990s, special-effects wizards began using computers to create even more life-like effects. In 1993, the dinosaurs of *Jurassic Park* jumped onto the screen, scaring audiences across America. *The Matrix* (1999) became a cult hit for its state-of-the-art special effects that used multiple cameras and slow motion.

Titanic was more than just a special-effects marvel. It rode to great popularity—and several Oscars—by bucking another trend of movies in the late 1900s. *Titanic* had spectacular effects of the ill-fated ship's collision with an iceberg and its subsequent sinking. The insides of the ship were recreated in stunning realism based on rigorous research, including recent undersea explo-

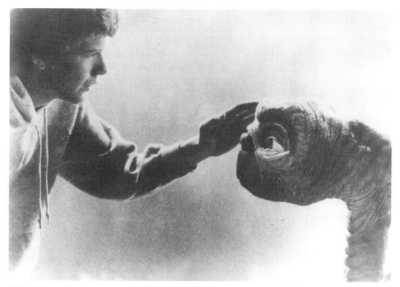

E.T.: The Extraterrestrial **was one of the most successful movies of all time.** (Movie Star News)

rations. The effects provided excitement; the romantic plot provided emotional drive to the story.

These blockbuster special effects movies, produced by major studios, cost huge amounts of money to make. Studios tried different methods to recoup those costs. They pushed to place the pictures on as many screens as possible. Many exhibitors had expanded quickly in the 1980s and 1990s, building huge new movie houses with multiple screens and comfortable seats. By 1995, the country had more than 26,000 indoor movie screens, up from just over 10,000 in 1971. All this construction cost a large amount of money. The exhibitors, then, also needed movies that were guaranteed to draw audiences, just as the studios did. Sequels were desirable because they brought a ready audience. Some stars became bankable box-office names. Exhibitors often scheduled promising movies on many of their screens in the same movie complex.

Studios also tried to recover costs of moviemaking by signing contracts with toymakers, clothing manufacturers, and fast-food restaurants. The toymakers made "action figures" of movie characters, timed to be sold when the movie was released. Clothing makers issued an array of apparel with logos and images from major movies. The restaurants became the exclusive distributors of movie-related prizes. They hoped to lure more customers—children and their parents—to their restaurants. If the movie was a hit, children kept coming back for more.

For some movies, all the planning and promotion paid off. A look at the chart, below, shows that nine of the ten highest-grossing films of all time were released in the 1980s and 1990s. The exception—the first *Star Wars* movie—was rereleased in the 1990s. Certainly these movies benefited from the higher ticket prices. But they also gained from the large number of screens and from exhibitors' decision to keep showing successful movies for months at a time. *Titanic*, the number-one grossing movie, was still in theaters nearly a year after its release.

Despite their efforts to promote movies, studio chiefs faced a troubling fact. Eighty percent or more of all movies made failed to make any money in theaters. The exhibitors quickly dropped the ones that did not draw big audiences in the first few weekends. Fortunately, producers had one other source of income—the video market. Videocassette recorders first reached mass audiences in the 1970s but became more important in the last two decades of the century. At first, movie studios worried that people watching videos at home would replace going to the movies.

Top Grossing Films

Top Grossing Films, as of 1999 (U.S. and Canada Only)

FILM	RELEASE YEAR	GROSS (MILLIONS)
Titanic	1997	$600.8
Star Wars: A New Hope [the original]	1977	461.0
Star Wars: The Phantom Menace	1999	431.0
E.T.	1982	399.8
Jurassic Park	1993	357.1
Forrest Gump	1994	329.7
The Lion King	1994	312.9
Star Wars: Return of the Jedi	1993	309.2
Independence Day	1996	306.2
Star Wars: The Empire Strikes Back	1980	290.3

Source: World Almanac and Book of Facts 2001

Soon, though, they realized that video fees could turn a box-office bust into a profitable movie. By the late 1990s, video sales and rentals generated $14 to $15 billion in revenue a year. That was more than double annual ticket sales of $6 billion.

Eight of the top ten videos sold were produced by the Disney studio, which focused its efforts on family movies that could be seen by children. In the 1960s, this studio had gone into a decline that lasted nearly two decades. New managers revitalized the company in the middle 1980s. Their new animated features once more made Disney a household name. A string of hits, from *The Little Mermaid* (1989) to *Hercules* (1997), followed. These movies showed some new thinking in the old studio. Earlier Disney successes had been firmly based in the European or Anglo American folk traditions. Some of the newer films reached out to the multicultural audience, with stories set in ancient Japan, the medieval Muslim world, and Africa.

The Written Word

The publishing industry was marked by a diversity of writers, many of them women. Popular African American women novelists included Toni Morison (who won a Nobel Prize in 1993) and Alice Walker. Latino writers included Sandra Cisneros and Cristina Garcia. Leslie Marmon Silko gave voice to Native Americans. Maxine Hong Kingston and Amy Tan produced well-crafted books about the Chinese American experience.

More established writers such as John Updike, Philip Roth, and John Irving continued to write important novels. Don DeLillo, Anne Tyler, and Jane Smiley moved into the ranks of respected fiction writers.

These works of literary fiction only formed a fraction of the book market, though. The novels that sold the most copies were adventure stories or romances. Stephen King's books emphasized the macabre and eerie. Tom Clancy told tales about spies and national security threats. John Grisham wrote books about the law that had interesting plot twists. Sue Grafton and others showed that mysteries were still a lively field. Danielle Steele wrote novels about glamorous people doing wicked things. Terry McMillan captured modern African American women's lifestyles.

One of the most interesting publishing phenomena came from England. A single mother, J. K. Rowling, wrote children's books about a young wizard named Harry Potter. The *Harry Potter* books gained a wide audience, with nearly 18 million copies of the first three books sold in the United States alone.

Bookselling changed in many ways in the late 1900s. The 1980s saw the birth of the "superstore." These giant bookstores held nearly 100,000 books—two or three times what could be found in a mall-based bookstore or independent store. The two big chains were Borders and Barnes & Noble. They opened superstores across the country—as many as two a week in the early 1990s. These stores made a comfortable space for readers. They had easy chairs where customers could test-read a new book. In the café, they could enjoy coffee, tea, and sweet breads.

The superstores were challenged starting in 1995, when Jeff Bezos launched the Web site Amazon.com. Bezos wanted to create a bookstore without a store. On his Internet site, people anywhere could visit to buy books and have them shipped fast. The Web site grew quickly, spurred by favorable news stories. By 2000, Amazon had earned $1 billion in yearly sales.

The World of Sports

Sports became increasingly visible in the late 1900s. Television's desire for programming to fill on-air time led networks to put more and more games on the air. To get those games, networks had to pay huge rights fees. Colleges could earn hundreds of thousands of dollars from these deals, especially in post-season games. Coaches felt pressure to make sure they reached those lucrative post-season appearances. Some skirted the rules. The National Collegiate Athletic Association (NCAA) policed the schools. Throughout the 1980s and 1990s, it was forced to place sanctions on several schools for breaking its rules.

Football was the big winner of the period. It passed baseball as the country's favorite professional sport. "Super Sunday," as the day of its championship Super Bowl game was called, became a national event. Streets were often deserted during the hours of the game because tens of millions of people were indoors watching it. Companies paid high fees to place commercials on the show so they could launch new products or revive sagging sales. Half-time shows became chances for music companies to promote their stars to the biggest audience possible.

Basketball also grew in popularity in these years. One reason was the arrival of two charismatic stars, Magic Johnson and Larry Bird, in the early 1980s. Then an even bigger star arrived. Michael Jordan joined the league in the late 1980s. In the 1990s, he led his Chicago Bulls team to six championships in eight years. (It might have been eight in eight, but Jordan retired briefly to try his hand at baseball.) Jordan's intensity and will to win was matched only by his grace and skill. He shrewdly cashed in on his fame by signing several marketing deals promoting products. Jordan became the most recognized athlete since boxer Muhammad Ali. People all over the world wanted to "be like Mike."

College basketball also rose in popularity in the late 1990s. The annual NCAA championship tournament, culminating in the "Final Four" weekend, attracted growing numbers of TV viewers. But some fans felt that the big money of the pro game damaged the college game. By the end of the century, the most talented players typically left college early so they could enter the professional league and begin collecting multimillion-dollar contracts sooner. Some players skipped college altogether. Kobe Bryant jumped from high school to the professional league. He was not the first, but his success made it clear that others would follow.

Baseball, meanwhile, was having serious financial problems. Baseball was the one pro sport with unfettered free agency. Players could cut all ties with their existing teams and sign a new contract with any other team. In other sports, rules put severe limits on players' ability to move, which kept salaries lower. In baseball—with no such limits—salaries skyrocketed. The result was to create severe imbalances in talent levels. Poor teams could develop young talent but then lost those players once they reached their free agency period. Rich teams could afford the soaring salaries of the best players. The wealthy Atlanta Braves won the National League championship five times in the 1990s. The even richer New York Yankees won three World Series in the same decade.

Baseball also suffered from two public relations disasters. The first was a scandal that touched one of the game's biggest stars. Pete Rose became the sport's all-time leading hitter in 1985. A few years later, though, he was punished for betting on baseball games. Rose was banned from any involvement in baseball for the rest of his life. The second problem was the players' strike of 1994–1995. The strike lasted for months, resulting in the cancellation of the 1994 World Series. When play resumed in 1995,

A professional skateboarder practices his moves. (CORBIS)

bitter fans stayed home in large numbers.

One new trend of the 1990s involved a new kind of sports, known as "extreme sports." Skateboarding was the first to take off, and children across America enjoyed twisting and turning as they launched into the air from the curved structures called half-pipes. Mountain biking was another favorite, as was snowboarding. Some of these extreme sports—extreme skiing and snow-boarding—found their way into the Olympics.

The games saw another change. More and more women were competing. The number of women's events grew over time, as did the number of athletes taking part. In 1991, the first Women's World Cup was held, with women's soccer teams from around the world competing. American women won the championship—a victory that they achieved again in 1999. Women also began to be seen in professional sports. A women's soccer league was formed and women, like men, were given the chance to make a living as pro athletes. Two professional basketball leagues were started for women as well. While these leagues struggled in their early years, they signaled that women's sports were becoming a mainstream phenomenon.

The spread of women's sports at the upper levels of Olympic and professional competition reflected the growth of women's sports. In the United States, much of this growth was due to Title IX, which was discussed in Chapter 2. The spread of women's sports could be seen not only in schools and colleges, but among children just beginning to compete. Soccer and softball fields across the country were home to young girls learning the basics of the sports.

There was also growth in participatory sports such as tennis, golf, swimming, and skiing. Many Americans were not content to sit at home and watch professional or college athletes compete on television. They wanted to take part themselves. This was part of the broader movement that promoted healthier lifestyles, including more exercise. Many people ran or biked. Others moved inside to fitness clubs, where they used high-tech weight machines to build muscle. Work in the weight-room became popular among many women as well as men.

Summary

The 1980s and 1990s, then, were a period of change. Changes in technology and taste changed how people were entertained and what performers they celebrated. The television industry changed radically in terms of the number of channels available and the variety of offerings. Music saw advances in the artistry shown in music videos and the growth in popularity of certain kinds of music. Moviemakers thrilled audiences with special effects thrillers both in theaters and at home, on video. Publishers and book sellers changed the way they went about the business of selling books. Sports saw the rise in popularity of some sports and a drop by others.

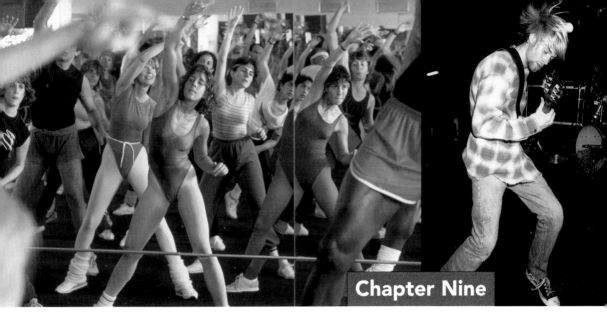

Chapter Nine

Fashions and Fads

The American people made a diverse nation in the late 1900s. As a result, the fashions and fads of the time showed great diversity. Many fashions spread up from the street instead of being handed down by the designers or high fashion—just as the hippie look of the 1960s had come to influence high fashion. Entertainment stars, especially those in the music industry, also had an influence on fashion. Fans of certain kinds of music adopted the clothing styles of performers, and as the popularity of the music grew so did the linked fashions. Different fashions came from different groups of people at different times, though, creating a myriad of looks. A major movement of the time— food fads—also reflected the diversity of the American people, as foods from many lands gained more popularity than they had enjoyed before.

During the 1980s, aerobics classes like this one became very popular. (CORBIS) Unlike rock stars of previous eras, Kurt Cobain (RIGHT), lead singer and songwriter of the influential rock band Nirvana paid little attention to the style, wearing flannel shirts and blue jeans. Ironically, largely because of his popularity, this "grunge" look became a popular fashion itself. (© S.I.N./CORBIS)

Clothing Fashions

The first fashion trend of the 1980s was the "preppy" look. Young people began to sport the classic look often seen in eastern private schools. This included khaki pants or plaid skirts, button-down shirts, sweaters in primary colors, and navy blazers. The preppy look was popular among "Yuppies," the nickname given to Young Urban Professionals. Many had found careers in business in the 1980s, where they wore "power suits." These traditional, conservative suits rejected the more colorful, flamboyant suits of the 1970s. Ties and lapels grew more narrow, and pinstripes became fashionable. As more and more women entered the business world, the power suit was adapted for them, often sporting large shoulder pads. At night, Yuppies enjoyed the varied night life of the cities where they settled. Then, they wore casual clothes.

The next trend was launched—in an unplanned way—by the movies. In the early 1980s, women were inspired by the movie *Flashdance* (1983). The film portrayed the gritty life of a young Pittsburgh woman who worked as a welder but dreamed of being a dancer. The heroine wore loose, off-the-shoulder sweaters over leotard tops along with tight pants and leg warmers.

The cool look of the television series *Miami Vice* spawned a male fashion craze. The series focused on two police officers fighting drug crimes in the Florida city. It featured the flashy colors of the tropics. The stars wore light, brightly colored suits. They abandoned collared shirts and ties for comfortable cotton t-shirts. The casual but hip look differed greatly from the power suit. While the colors darkened after the decline of the series, the t-shirt-and-suit combination stayed popular to the end of the century.

Some young people rejected both the preppy look and the *Flashdance* style. They chose the look originally sported by punk-rock bands of the late 1970s. Punk included bizarre hair styles. Some people shaved their heads. Others kept their hair, but dyed it bright purple or orange. They also shaped it in strange ways, often with spiky peaks sticking in several different directions. Some shaved the sides, leaving a row of tall spikes along the center of their heads. Punk clothing was distinctive, too. It was marked by torn t-shirts and jeans with holes. Most distinctive were the safety pins stuck in clothing—or in the wearer's body. The punk look eventually faded. Piercing, though, continued to appeal to young people through the end of the 1990s. Eventually, safety pins were abandoned. Ears, noses, lips, tongues, and navels were adorned, instead, with costume jewelry. The rich and famous, of course, decorated their pierced selves with expensive gems. Even pro athletes, often concerned with their image as powerful males, began to wear diamond-studded earrings.

Another new look from the street came out of rap music. Rap

was linked to a culture called "hip-hop." This movement was born in African American city neighborhoods. Along with rap, hip-hop was linked to graffiti painting and a new style of dance called "break dancing." Athletic and vigorous, break dancing was marked by complex spins, twists, and other moves carried out in a small space. But hip-hop culture was more than art, dance, and music. It also contributed new clothing styles. That style included extremely baggy pants, bare midriffs, and heavy gold jewelry. The outfit was often topped by a baseball cap worn backward or by a woolen ski cap. On their feet, the hip-hop generation wore large sneakers, often with laces untied.

The hip-hop look quickly spread from the inner cities to the white suburbs. Across America, baggy pants and low-slung jeans were in. Hip-hop produced another fad in body adornment—tattoos. Young people flocked to tattoo parlors to have words or pictures drawn on their skin. A few unfortunates decorated themselves with the names of their current flame. When the relationships ended, the tattoos, alas, remained.

Grunge music provided another new fashion look. This look was marked by flannel shirts, military-style shoes, and knit caps popular in the Northwest.

High Fashion

Top fashion designers placed a strong emphasis on showing the body. The fitness craze of the 1970s had continued into the 1980s. Young adults jogged, played squash, biked, and did aerobics. Weight training became popular, not only for men but also for women. After all that work, many people wanted to show off their firm, muscled bodies. Form-fitting fabrics became widespread. So, too, did scoop-necked tops, short skirts, and brief shorts.

Top fashion designers took the athletic look in two directions. Evening clothes for women became very revealing, with low cut fronts, low slung backs, and cut-outs that revealed the wearer's skin. At the same time, many designers pushed a new category of clothing called "activewear." Activewear was comfortable and flexible. Some pieces looked like exercise clothes. Others followed more traditional cuts but used soft, comfortable fabrics

An outfit from 1987 by designer Geoffrey **Beene** (Dover Publications)

that let the wearer move freely.

Even underwear became high fashion in the late 1900s. In the early 1980s, designer Calvin Klein began to promote new lines of cotton underwear. The ads promoting these new products featured models in daring poses. What made the campaign most unusual was that it was promoting men's underwear. Dramatic photos of male models in their underwear was a fashion first. Soon after, Klein followed with a line of women's cotton underwear styled similar to the men's line. One retailer took a different approach to women's underclothing. A new chain of stores called Victoria's Secret began to appear in malls across the country. Its designs emphasized the female figure and used bold colors.

Singers Madonna and Cyndi Lauper popularized another trend in underwear—wearing it on top of, not underneath, clothing.

Many designer clothes carried the designer's logo. The movement had begun with designer jeans in the 1970s. In the late 1900s, designers splashed identifying symbols on pants, tops, sweaters, and jackets. Clothing became a way of declaring allegiance with something or someone. Millions wore t-shirts and hats that proclaimed the name of the company they worked for, the group they belonged to, or the sports team they rooted for. Jerseys, hats, and jackets that carried team logos became part of everyday wear. Baseball hats became the headgear of choice across the country. By the end of the 1990s, though, western hats had come in style for men.

Toys and Games

A popular pastime of the 1980s was a board game imported from Canada. Called "Trivial Pursuit," the game asked two to six players to compete in their knowledge of current events and popular culture. Reaching the United States in 1983, the game had more than 20 million sets sold in just two years. Several spin-offs were produced. They focused on special topics such as Disney characters and movies or popular music.

Video and computer games were even more popular. The first video game, "Pong" issued by the company Atari, had appeared in the 1970s. In the early 1980s, the big hits were "Asteroids," "Pac-Man" and its spin-off "Ms. Pac-Man," and "Space Invaders." All were played on bulky machines that were expensive. Very quickly, though, the computers driving the games became faster and more powerful. Soon, game companies produced smaller, cheaper game-playing equipment that could be used at home. And people gobbled them up. Game companies saw sales—and profits—soar. But many thousands of video-game arcades that had been set up in malls across the country lost business and had to close.

Two other game fads generated interest in the 1990s. Pogs were small, flat disks made of cardboard and decorated with colorful patterns or pictures. Children collected and traded them. They also enjoyed playing with "Magic" cards. These card sets played on the popularity of books and movies involving swords and sorcery. Cards pictured different kinds of creatures, each with special strengths and weaknesses. Children played their decks against each other as they tried to control a mythical world.

Many popular toys and games were linked to successful television shows or movies. Shows like the *Teenage Mutant Ninja Turtles* and *Power Rangers* inspired action figures that earned high sales. George Lucas, the creator of the Star Wars movies, made hundreds of millions of dollars by licensing the movies' characters to different toymakers.

Masaya Nakamura, creator of the popular video arcade game, takes a turn at Pac-Man in 1982. He told reporters at the time that he was happy about the global success of his creation, but a "little concerned about the way some young people play so much." (© Bettmann/CORBIS)

Food Fashions

American eating habits showed many changes in the late 1900s. Fast-food restaurants became more popular as working parents had less time to cook after in a full day's work. To broaden their appeal, the restaurants experimented with their menus. McDonalds, the biggest chain during this period, tried to market a newer, low-calorie burger in the early 1990s. It also began selling salads and grilled meats that were lower in calories. A new fast-food chain, Subway, rose to popularity selling low-calorie sandwiches made from low-fat meats, vegetables, and freshly baked breads. Many restaurants sported special symbols beside some dishes that met standards set by the American Heart Association as promoting healthy hearts. At the same time, many fast-food chains began "super-sizing" their dishes, giving people more fries or larger drinks for just a few pennies extra.

Critics complained that super-sized meals helped lead to the fattening of America. Public health officials openly worried that too many people were overweight, which led to heart disease, circulation problems, and diabetes. These officials also pointed with alarm to the rising rates of heaviness among children. Other trends contributed to the fact that many were gaining weight. More people than in earlier eras had office or sales jobs; fewer engaged in physical labor. As a result, they used less energy in their normal activities. This relative inactivity continued at night, when many people found entertainment by watching television or similar activities.

While this trend was worrisome, the exercise fads that had begun in the 1970s still continued. A large number of Americans were very careful with their health. They ate whole foods and focused on low-fat, low-sugar diets. Many people shopped at stores that offered organically grown foods, which they felt were healthier.

For Americans who wished to lose weight, doctors, nutritionists, and health experts offered a range of weight-loss diet choices. Programs like Weight Watchers tried to promote balanced, low-fat, high-nutrient diets reinforced by group meetings where people could receive support for their efforts to lose weight. The Atkins diet promoted a diet high in protein and fat but low in carbohydrates, the nutrients found in pasta, rice, and bread. Others tried still other approaches. These different diets passed into and out of fashion. Most experts agreed that anyone who really wanted to lose weight needed to follow two simple rules: eat less and exercise more.

American eating habits were changing in other ways as the twentieth century closed. A higher percentage of Americans than ever before had been to college. More than ever before had traveled to other countries. Immigrants were coming in greater numbers from Asia and Latin America. These trends contributed to a new openness to food from other countries.

The interest in greater variety in cooking had begun in the

1960s and 1970s. That's when Julia Child introduced Americans to French cooking with her popular television cooking show. Italian food also gained in popularity in these decades, as did Chinese. In the 1980s and 1990s, Americans found a number of new ethnic cuisines appealing. Thai and Cuban restaurants opened across the country. Many people began to crave Japanese sushi and sashimi. Mexican food was also very popular. Mexican chain restaurants popped up across the country. In addition, smaller family run restaurants opened in many cities. In a clear signal that Mexican food had arrived, salsa passed ketchup as the country's top-selling condiment food. Even coffee developed a new style. A chain of coffee houses called Starbucks came out of the Pacific Northwest to sweep the country. It sold high-quality American-style coffee and creamy concoctions made with European espresso.

Summary

The 1980s and 1990s were a fast-paced era, full of many changes. This was true in fashions and fads, as in other areas of American life. Clothing had many different looks in these decades, as no one style dominated the period. Instead, different combinations became popular at different times—and sometimes several looks could be seen in American cities at the same time.

Food trends of the late 1900s revealed how Americans' lives had changed during the twentieth century. The growth of gourmet foods showed the country's greater economic connection with other countries around the world. People could easily enjoy cheeses from Europe and fruits and vegetables during the winter from South America. The openness to foods from other lands also reflected the rising levels of education in the country. People were more interested in new experiences. The popularity of these foods revealed peoples' generally higher income levels. A larger number of people than before could afford more expensive foods. Finally, the spread of new ethnic restaurants highlighted the growing diversity of the American people.

Bibliography

Ahearn, Robert. *America Today: American Heritage Illustrated History of the United States, Volume 18*. New York: Choice Publishing, 1988.

Ciment, James. *The Young People's History of the United States*. New York: Barnes and Noble Books, 1998.

Derks, Scott. *Working Americans, 1880–1999*. Lakeville, CT: Greyhouse Publishing, 2000.

Craats, Rennay. *History of the 1980's*. Calgary, Canada and Mankato, MN: Weigl Educational Publishers, 2001.

Craats, Rennay. *History of the 1990's*. Calgary, Canada and Mankato, MN: Weigl Educational Publishers, 2001.

Groner, Alex. *The History of American Business and Industry*. New York: American Heritage, 1972.

Harvey, Edmund H. *Our Glorious Century*. Pleasantville, NY: Reader's Digest Association, 2000.

Mintz, Steven and Susan Kellogg. *Domestic Revolutions: A Social History of American Family Life*. New York: The Free Press, 1988.

Weiss, Suzanne E. *The American Story: Who, What, When, Where and Why of Our Nation's Heritage*. Pleasantville, NY: Reader's Digest Association, 2000.

Index

Note: Page numbers in *italics* refer to illustrations.

See also education
child support, 34
China, trade with, 68-69
cigarette smoking, teenage, 28
Civil Rights Act, 43
Clean Air Act, 108
climate change, 108
Clinton, Bill, 36, 39
    conservative policies of, 17, 31, 38
    economy and, 17, 65-66
    education policy of, 52, 53
    election of 1992, 9, 16-17, 65
    election of 1996, 11
    health care plan of, 34
    impeachment of, 11, 18
    Lewinsky scandal, 17-18
    trade policy of, 69
    volunteerism and, 36-37
    welfare reform and, 31
    Whitewater investigation of, 18
Clinton, Hillary Rodham, 18, 34
cloning, 105
clothing styles, 129-132
Cold War, end of, 9-10
colleges and universities
    affirmative action in, 47-48, 60
    African Americans in, 60
    costs of, 61-62
    distance learning, 62
    graduation rate, 49
    older students in, 61
    sports in, 125, 126
    women in, 60-61
Columbine High School shootings, 58-59, 59
Commonwealth of Independent States (CIS), 10
communications technology, 21, 79-80
communism, collapse of, 9-10
computer games, 132-133
computer industry, 74-75
computer technology
    advances in, 9, 21
    in education, 49-50, 53, 62
    health problems related to, 80, 81
    privacy issue in, 80-81
    in workplace, 65, 77-81
    Y2K bug and, 104
    See also Internet
Congress
    Clinton impeachment in, 11, 18
    gun control in, 40-41
    NAFTA and, 69
    Republican control of, 10, 38-39
    toxic chemical cleanup in, 110
    welfare reform in, 31
conservatives, 15, 31
    on abortion, 46-47
    in Congress, 38-39
    on government regulation, 37-38
    on social problems, 38
    on welfare reform, 31
Consumer Price Index (CPI), 6
consumer spending, 6, 64

Contract with America, 38-39
Contras, 15
Coolidge, Calvin, 88
country music, 121
crime
    hate crime, 44, 90
    rate, 39-40
    school shootings, 27, 41, 58-61
    violent, 41
    See also bombings

D
day care, 26
death, leading causes of, 106
death penalty, 40
defense spending, 5, 15, 64-65
demographic trends, 18-20, 23
disabled people, civil rights for, 42-43
discrimination. *See* prejudice and discrimination
diseases
    asthma, 107
    cancer, 106
    HIV/AIDS, 32, 44-45, 106-107
    leading causes of death, 106
distance learning, 62
divorce, 22, 23, 25, 34, 91-92
DNA, 104-105
Dole, Robert, 11
Dow Jones Industrial Average, 71
Drexler, K. Eric, 113
drug use, 27, 39-40

E
Eastern Orthodox church, 92
eating habits, 133-135
e-commerce, 75
economy
    conservative thinkers on, 37-38
    globalization, 67, 70-71
    growth periods, 5-7, 16, 17, 65-67
    in recession, 16, 64, 65
    stock market boom, 71-73
    world's largest economies, 68
education
    alternative assessment approach in, 50-51
    bilingual, 56
    charter schools, 55, 55-56
    computers in classroom, 49-50, 53
    equal opportunity in, 46
    funding gap in, 52-53
    home schooling, 30
    physical deterioration and overcrowding, 51
    preschool, 57-58
    in private schools, 56-57
    privatization of, 54-55, 55
    religious fundamentalists and, 93-94
    in segregated schools, 53
    sex education, 27
    social promotion in, 54
    technology gap in, 53
    violence in schools, 27, 41, 58-60
    vouchers, 57